MATHEMATICS AND THE LAWS OF NATURE
DEVELOPING THE LANGUAGE OF SCIENCE

D0005400

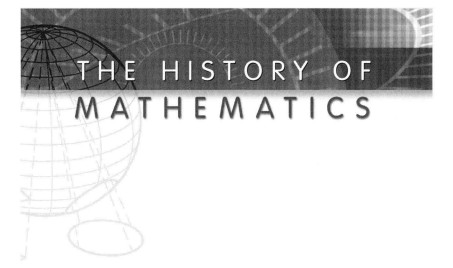

MATHEMATICS AND
THE LAWS OF NATURE

DEVELOPING THE LANGUAGE OF SCIENCE

John Tabak, Ph.D.

Facts On File, Inc.

MATHEMATICS AND THE LAWS OF NATURE: Developing the Language of Science

Facts On File, Inc.
132 West 31st Street
New York NY 10001

Library of Congress Cataloging-in-Publication Data

Tabak, John.
   Mathematics and the laws of nature: developing the language of science / John Tabak.
     p. cm. — (History of mathematics)
   Includes bibliographical references and index.
   ISBN 0-8160-4957-2 (acid-free paper)
   1. Mathematics—History. 2. Science—History. I. Title.
   QA21.T22 2004
   510'.9—dc222003016961

Facts On File books are available at special discounts when purchased in bulk quantities for businesses, associations, institutions, or sales promotions. Please call our Special Sales Department in New York at (212) 967-8800 or (800) 322-8755.

You can find Facts On File on the World Wide Web at http://www.factsonfile.com

Text design by David Strelecky
Cover design by Kelly Parr
Illustrations by Patricia Meschino

Printed in the United States of America

MP FOF 10 9 8 7 6 5 4 3 2 1

This book is printed on acid-free paper.

To George Baker. He is a law unto himself.

CONTENTS

ACKNOWLEDGMENTS

The author is deeply appreciative of Frank K. Darmstadt, Executive Editor, for his many helpful suggestions and of Dorothy Cummings, Project Editor, for the insightful work that she did editing this volume.

Special thanks to Penelope Pillsbury and the staff of the Brownell Library, Essex Junction, Vermont, for their extraordinary help with the many difficult research questions that arose during the preparation of this book.

INTRODUCTION

NATURAL LAWS

What is a law of nature? Scientists and philosophers began asking that question thousands of years ago. The answer has changed and changed and changed again. It is not clear when people first began to look for the fundamental principles that govern the physical world, but we do know that the search for these principles is at least as old as the written word. The people of Mesopotamia, one of the earliest civilizations with a written language, seemed quite comfortable with the idea that there were patterns that somehow underlay the world around them. Furthermore they clearly believed that with effort they could identify and describe those patterns. They were remarkably successful.

Thousands of years after the Mesopotamians began writing about their research into nature, the question of what constitutes a law of nature remains only partially answered. Apart from the answer, the meaning of the question itself has undergone regular revisions over the intervening centuries. Although there is currently widespread agreement on several points, much is still open for debate. The reason is simple. The question, What is a natural law? remains something of a moving target. The more we learn about science and mathematics, the deeper our appreciation for the old question becomes, and the less satisfied we are with the old answers. A little research at a library or on the Internet reveals a long list of papers, some by eminent philosophers and scientists, about the definition of laws of nature.

The discovery of new laws of nature is a pursuit that scientists in all parts of the world enjoy, but scientists do not simply collect natural laws as a successful athlete might collect trophies. Trophies, once earned, are just keepsakes. They collect dust. Natural laws, on the other hand, are important to science because natural laws are *used*. They are used to generate new scientific discoveries and to clarify old ones. Natural laws, mathematically expressed, form the basis of a great deal of scientific research.

The discovery of a new natural law is as infrequent as it is important. In fact most successful scientists never discover a single natural law. Instead they spend their working life researching how particular phenomena in their chosen field—whether it be geology, meteorology, or astronomy, to name just a few examples—can be understood as consequences of a small number of very general laws of nature. These laws enable them to develop a clearer understanding of the phenomena in which they have an interest and to make predictions based on these very general principles. Technology, too, depends on a clear understanding of the laws of nature. Natural laws enable scientists and engineers to understand and exploit physical processes more efficiently as they attempt to manipulate information, mass, and energy.

Laws of nature are sometimes described as generalizations of our experience. One commonly cited example of this idea is the law of conservation of mass. The law of conservation of mass states that mass is neither created nor destroyed during a chemical reaction. This law is sometimes said to have been "proved" by repeated careful measurements of masses before and after chemical reactions. This is false. Because the law of conservation of mass applies to all chemical reactions, not just to the ones that have been observed, it *cannot be proved* by any specific set of experiments. No experiments can rule out the existence of other experiments in which the law of conservation of mass is violated. The assertion that mass is conserved had to be based on more than what had been observed in a lab. It was a deep insight into the nature of matter.

In this book we see that laws of nature are usually more than generalizations of our ordinary experience, and, in fact, most generalizations, scientific or otherwise, are not laws of nature at all. To understand some of the very specific ways that simple generalizations differ from natural laws, we can look at physics, the first field in which natural laws were successfully formulated. In physics one property that natural laws have is that they are *invariant*.

In physics a property of a system is called invariant in space if it is true everywhere. In other words, if we perform the same experiment under the same conditions we always observe the same result. This is true whether we perform the experiment in Canada or Cuba, Earth or Mars. The laws of nature, which are what we use to predict the outcome of our experiment accurately, should be independent of our position on Earth or, more generally, of our position anywhere in the universe—from star to star or galaxy to galaxy. A natural law is not just valid in our neighborhood. It is valid everywhere.

Natural laws are also invariant with respect to time. The same experiment performed under the same conditions should give the same result whether we perform it today or tomorrow. And if we read of an experiment performed long ago, we should be able to duplicate the results of that experiment ourselves today. Time changes; natural laws do not.

Every natural law has its limitations, however. Each natural law is a *description* of the way nature behaves. Like any description, a natural law is necessarily an incomplete description. It is accurate when applied to processes and phenomena provided those processes and phenomena occur under carefully defined conditions, but there is no one-size-fits-all natural law in any scientific field.

In this book we take special interest in the mathematical expression of the laws of nature. Because mathematics is a language of great precision, understanding the meaning of a law once it has been expressed mathematically is often much easier. Moreover, some of the most important advances in mathematics have occurred in response to attempts by scientists to express laws of nature in a mathematical way. Likewise discoveries by mathematicians have enabled scientists to understand better the mathematical basis of laws of nature. Finally, by examining how mathematics and science have evolved together, we can develop a fuller appreciation for both. The history of natural laws is a story of how science (and to a large extent, the modern world!) became what it is. It is a story of imagination and insight, contemplation and discovery.

1

NATURE AS GEOMETRY

Five thousand years ago on a hot, flat, largely treeless expanse of land, a land devoid of stone and other building materials, the people whom we know as Sumerians began to build a civilization. They irrigated land. They built cities. They built schools and developed one of the first written languages in history, called cuneiform. Because their land was difficult to defend against military attack, and because the city-states in the area frequently attacked one another, the political history of Sumer is complicated and bloody. Despite the turmoil, however, their culture endured. Over time Sumerian culture became the foundation for a larger culture. Slowly the culture of the Sumerians was absorbed and transformed into the culture of Mesopotamia.

Of special importance to us are the written records of the Mesopotamians. The system of writing that the Sumerians began, a system characterized by imprints on clay tablets, was slowly changed and enriched by those who succeeded them. Long after the people of Mesopotamia ceased speaking the Sumerian language they continued to incorporate elements of the Sumerian written language into their own written language. The last known cuneiform texts—which concern astronomy—date from the first century C.E. That is 3,000 years of cuneiform writing! Over the next 2,000 years Mesopotamian civilization was largely forgotten. Mesopotamian culture was eventually rediscovered in the 19th century, when archaeological excavations unearthed and catalogued hundreds of thousands of clay tablets. In time scholars translated the tablets and found tables of numbers that were used in mathematical computations, histories of military campaigns, letters from

This seventh-century B.C.E. cuneiform tablet is a copy of a 17th-century B.C.E. tablet containing observations of the planet Venus. (© Copyright The British Museum)

students to parents, inventories of goods, lists of laws, and records of astronomical observations. It was an astonishingly complete record of one of history's earliest and longest-lasting civilizations.

The Ancient Sky

The Mesopotamians were avid astronomers. They seem to have watched the heavens almost continuously for thousands of years, carefully documenting their observations in the form of astronomical diaries, forming theories, and making predictions. Through Mesopotamian astronomy we can see one of the earliest attempts to develop a system of "laws" for the purpose of describing natural phenomena.

Mesopotamian astronomers concentrated on the problem of predicting future astronomical phenomena. They were less interested in why things occurred than they were in knowing what was going to happen next. Making these astronomical predictions successfully required a high level of social organization. For many years their method of learning about astronomy emphasized examining the records of past astronomical observations for clues about future events. To do this they required good educational institutions, a written language, skilled observers, and careful record keepers. They required stable institutions that could collect and preserve records over the course of many generations. Many cultural and educational barriers had to be overcome before they could begin a systematic search for the laws of nature. To understand the kind of astronomical predictions in which the Mesopotamians were interested (and in which they excelled), knowing a little about how they understood the sky is helpful.

The modern reader needs patience and imagination to appreciate what it was those astronomers were observing, not just because we are unfamiliar with Mesopotamian science, but also because we are unfamiliar with the night sky. In the days before electric lights the night skies shimmered with the light of a multitude of stars, both bright and dim. Nebulae were visible to the naked eye. A brilliant night sky was a familiar sight to people all over the planet. Today most of us have rarely, if ever, seen a truly dark, clear sky. We have never seen a nebula except as a picture in a book or an image on the Web. We cannot. The light of most of these objects is lost in the glare of streetlights and headlights, stoplights and illuminated advertisements. We live in a different world. We live under a different night sky.

But anyone in Earth's Northern Hemisphere who spends a few hours out of doors, on a clear night, away from bright lights, care-

The bright streaks are star trails, the apparent paths of stars across the night sky. (Rob Crandall/The Image Works)

fully observing the stars, notices that some stars seem to move across the sky in great arcs while one star seems to remain in place. That one star is Polaris, the North Star. The farther in the sky a star appears to be from Polaris, the larger an arc it makes. Stars that appear close to Polaris travel in small circles, each centered on Polaris. The larger arcs dip below the horizon, so over the course of the evening, stars farther from Polaris may well disappear from view. If, however, we could trace a large arc over the horizon and all the way around the sky, we would find that these stars, too, trace large circles centered on Polaris.

When we see stars move across the night sky in circular arcs, we know that they only appear to move. We know that their apparent motion is due to the revolution of the Earth about its axis. Because the stars are many trillions of miles away from us, their actual motions are too small for us to notice. But whether the Earth rotates and the stars are fixed, or whether the stars orbit a fixed Earth, the view from Earth is the same: We observe the stars apparently orbiting steadily around the Earth in great circular arcs. The Mesopotamians studied the motion of the stars under the belief that the stars themselves moved. Of course they got it wrong, but it was (and remains) an "obvious" explanation for what any of us can observe nightly.

If one believes, as the Mesopotamians did, that the stars revolve around Earth, then there are seven astronomical objects, visible to the naked eye, that warrant special attention. These seven objects are exceptional because they do not move across the sky in the same way as the rest of the stars. Some of them even seem to remain in place for days or weeks at a time and then reverse course for a while. They also change speed on their journey across the night sky. These exceptional objects are Mercury, Venus, Mars, Jupiter, Saturn, the Moon, and the Sun. The Mesopotamians were aware of all seven of these astronomical objects.

For a modern reader the inclusion of the Sun in the list may be a little puzzling, but the Mesopotamians tracked the motion of the Sun across the sky just as they tracked the motions of the planets. This is because relative to the background stars, the Sun appears to change position in the sky. The Mesopotamians, as we

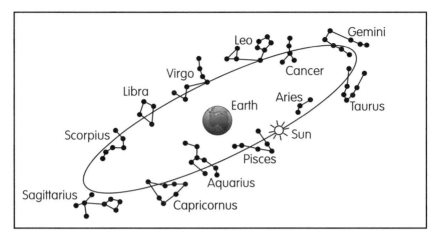

Depending on the relative positions of the Earth and Sun, the position of the Sun in the ecliptic appears to change.

do, organized stars into constellations. They made careful observations of the position of each star in each constellation. They observed that near sunset at a particular time of year a certain constellation would be near the horizon as the Sun set. As a consequence the Sun would lie almost inside the constellation. (The constellation near which the Sun set depended on the time of year.) With each succeeding day the constellation in question would be a little nearer the horizon at sunset. Each day it would remain visible for an even briefer period of time before it, too, sank below the horizon. Eventually the constellation that they had been observing would not be visible at all. It would be lost in the glare of the Sun because it would be too near the Sun to be visible. At this point the Sun would be "in" the constellation. The process would then repeat for a different constellation. In this way they noted that the Sun moved from constellation to constellation. The pattern was always the same. The set of constellations through which the Sun moved was the same from year to year. We call the apparent path of the Sun across the sky the ecliptic. The Mesopotamians, too, recognized the ecliptic as the path that the Sun followed across the sky through this very special set of constellations.

Early Mesopotamian astronomers made similar observations of the Moon and the planets. Each clear night they made a record of the position of each object in the night sky. They knew that all seven of the exceptional astronomical objects, the Sun, Moon, Mercury, Venus, Mars, Jupiter, and Saturn, were always to be seen—if they were visible at all—in a narrow band centered on the ecliptic. Of more immediate interest to Mesopotamian astronomers were questions about the first appearance of a planet in the night sky and where in the sky that planet could be found six months or a year in the future. Astronomical phenomena formed a very important part of Mesopotamian culture.

Recording the Stars to Predict the Future

Why were these observations important? The Mesopotamians believed that they would be able to predict earthly events if they could predict the motions of the heavens. The idea that astronomical phenomena and terrestrial phenomena were linked provided much of the impetus for their astronomical work. Some celestial predictions turned out to be much easier than others. Predicting the motions of the stars is a relatively easy process, because they are very regular. To make accurate predictions of stellar motions—to be able, for example, to predict the date on which a star will first become visible at the horizon—one needs only an accurate calendar. Devising an accurate calendar is, to be sure, hard work, but it is the only hard problem involved. Almost as soon as the Mesopotamians had devised a reasonably accurate calendar, they were able to predict with reasonable precision the first appearance of any star of interest in the night sky from one year to the next. Their calendar was not as accurate as ours, so their predictions about the first appearance in the night sky of one star or another were not—by our standards, at least—especially accurate. Still they seemed satisfied with the results. The movements of the stars are extremely regular, so small inaccuracies in the calendar led to small inaccuracies in the predictions.

Predicting the motions of the Sun, Moon, and planets was more challenging, because the motions of these objects are far less regular than the motions of the stars. It was with the goal of predicting the future positions of these "exceptional" objects that the Mesopotamians devoted considerable time, energy, and creativity.

For early Mesopotamian astronomers the key to predicting the future motions of the Moon, Sun, and planets was to be found in the past. For many centuries these astronomers based their predictions on an analysis of carefully maintained records of previous positions of these objects through the night sky. The amount of work involved in making and maintaining these records over many centuries was extraordinary, but for a very long time they had no other option. A good example of how they accomplished this type of astronomical analysis is their study of the planet Saturn.

Saturn orbits the Sun along an elliptical path, a path that resembles a slightly flattened circle. By astronomical standards Saturn is not very far from Earth, so its motion relative to the background stars is clearly visible. If we watch Saturn regularly we can see it move from constellation to constellation, always remaining in a band of sky called the zodiac. (Saturn's path, as well as the paths taken by all the other planets through the night sky, fall within the zodiac.)

If we could observe Saturn's motions from the Sun itself, describing its path across the background stars would be a fairly simple matter. Accurate predictions are complicated by the fact that we are viewing Saturn from Earth, which is itself a moving platform. Our planet moves rapidly around the Sun even as it rotates on its own axis. What makes our observations even more difficult to interpret is that we have no feeling of motion. Although Earth travels hundreds of millions of miles through space each year, we have no physical sense of this motion, and so our observations of Saturn are not easy to understand.

To see the problem, imagine that you are in a car traveling parallel with a train. If the car is traveling faster than the train *and if you have no feeling of motion*, the train can appear to be backing up. If you are traveling a little more slowly than the train, the train will appear to be moving slowly forward, even though your car and the train may both be moving rapidly forward. Add to this the complication that Saturn and Earth both travel curved paths—and Earth, having the inside track, moves much faster about the Sun than Saturn—and you begin to see the difficulties faced by the Mesopotamians.

Saturn's apparent motions relative to the background stars can be divided into three types. Generally Saturn moves eastward along the zodiac, the same direction that the Sun moves. The technical term for this is *prograde* motion. Sometimes, however, Saturn's apparent motion across the sky halts; from Earth Saturn appears stationary. This period of motionlessness can last for a few weeks. This is a called a *station* of Saturn. Finally, there are times when Saturn reverses direction and appears to travel backwards (westward) through the zodiac. This is called *retrograde* motion. (Saturn, of course, never stops or changes direction. These motions appear to occur because we are observing Saturn from a moving platform.)

The Mesopotamians observed these motions and stations and recorded them, but they were especially interested in where the motions and stations occurred in relation to the stars. To the Mesopotamians a planetary cycle was not complete until the planet repeated *the same sequence of motions and stations in the same parts of the zodiac as it had previously.* In other words a cycle ended when Saturn went through the same sequence of stations, prograde motions, and retrograde motions, and each part of the sequence occurred against the same backdrop of stars that had been previously observed. In the case of Saturn these cycles are fairly long. To complete one trip around the zodiac, Saturn requires about 29 years, but to complete one entire cycle of stations, prograde motions, and retrograde motions (as the Mesopotamians understood it), Saturn requires not 29 years but 59 years. It was necessary, therefore, to observe Saturn for a few generations in order to observe a single cycle. That is why the astronomical diaries maintained by the Mesopotamian astronomers were important: Many Mesopotamian astronomers did not live long enough to observe even one cycle of Saturn.

What is true of Saturn is true of the other planets as well. The Mesopotamians had scribes whose job it was to watch the heavens nightly and to keep records of what they observed. These records were then copied neatly, compiled, and analyzed for patterns. The result was that they were able to identify cyclic behavior in all of the planets' motions. This enabled them to compile predictions of earthly events based on the predicted behavior of the planets. For example, they detected an 18-year cycle for the Moon (which was important for predicting eclipses), an eight-year cycle for Venus, and a 46-year cycle for Mercury. They detected two distinct cyclic periods in the motions of Jupiter and Mars. Some contemporary scholars believe these multiple cycles were related to the motions of Jupiter relative to the stars and its motions relative to the planets themselves. Jupiter was found to follow 71- and 83-year cycles. Mars was found to follow 47- and 79-year cycles.

The Mesopotamians combined these cycles to produce something called a goal-year text. The goal-year text was a set of predictions of astronomical phenomena for the coming year. Here is how they did it: To predict the motions of Mercury, they consulted the records on Mercury from 46 years earlier because they knew that Mercury has a 46- year cycle. To predict the motions of Venus they consulted the records on Venus from eight years previous because Venus has an eight-year cycle. The Moon has an 18-year cycle so they consulted records from 18 years earlier, and because Jupiter has 71- and 83-year cycles they consulted the records on Jupiter from 71 and 83 years previous, and so on. They had discovered that past patterns of astronomical events could be used to predict future astronomical events. In this way they obtained reasonably good predictions of the behavior of all heavenly bodies with an absolute minimum of mathematics or theoretical insight. For the Mesopotamians, predicting the behavior of the heavens was a straightforward matter of observation, record keeping, and data analysis.

The Astronomical Calculations

One striking point about the astronomical diaries that the Mesopotamians kept night after night and year after year is that there were a lot of cloudy nights. Perhaps this was one reason that they eventually turned away from direct observation and toward the computation of the positions of astronomical objects. Perhaps they felt that if they could not see an object's position, they could at least compute it. Whatever the reason, the Mesopotamians gradually developed more mathematical methods of describing the motions of the Moon, Sun, and five known planets. Over time they developed multiple mathematical systems for predicting the positions of astronomical objects. These systems required the user to know a small number of facts about the object of interest and be able to solve certain algebraic equations. No longer did these early astronomers require generations of record keepers because they no longer depended so heavily on past observations. To understand what they did and the difficulties that they overcame, we examine their method of predicting the position of the Sun along the ecliptic. First, however, let us review a few facts about solar and planetary motions.

When we picture Earth revolving around the Sun, many of us imagine our planet moving along a circular orbit. That is almost correct, but Earth's orbit is not circular. It is *almost* circular. Earth's orbital path is an ellipse, and because it is elliptic, part of its orbital path lies closer to the Sun and part lies farther away. Changes in the Earth-Sun distance are relatively small when compared to Earth's average distance to the Sun. Nevertheless these changes in the distance from Earth to the Sun have an effect on Earth's orbital speed: The closer Earth is to the Sun, the faster it goes. (This fact was not discovered until the 17th century.) The difference between Earth's greatest and least distances from the Sun is small, so the velocity changes are also small—but not so small that the Mesopotamians were unable to detect them. What the Mesopotamians noticed is that the apparent speed of the Sun across the sky is not constant. Because we observe the universe from a moving platform, the apparent speed of the Sun through the zodiac is a reflection of the speed of the Earth around the Sun. The faster Earth goes, the faster the Sun seems to move against the background stars when viewed from Earth. All the Mesopotamians needed to predict the future position of the Sun was the present position of the Sun and an equation that described how the "Sun's speed" changed as it moved along the ecliptic. These observations gave rise to one of the very earliest mathematical models in history.

To understand the Mesopotamian mathematical model of the Sun's motions and to get a little experience analyzing mathematical models, suppose that the Sun moves along the ecliptic at constant speed. The advantage of such a simple model is that it is easy to use. The disadvantage is that it is not very accurate. (In mathematical modeling there is usually a trade-off between accuracy and ease of use. What we gain in one we lose in the other.) If we assume that the Sun moves along the ecliptic at constant speed, there is a substantial difference between our computed position and the Sun's actual position at certain times during the year: Sometimes the Sun is ahead of its computed position, sometimes behind it. Of course if we found the correct constant speed then we could correctly predict that at the end of the year the Sun would be right back where it started, but we knew that before we began. A constant-speed model of the Sun's motion is not very useful.

The Mesopotamians knew that one way to improve this simple, not-very-accurate constant-velocity approach is to divide the ecliptic into two zones, a fast zone and a slow zone. They still imagined that the Sun traveled at a constant velocity in each zone, but the speed they used depended on the zone where the Sun was. This approach decreases the error between the Sun's computed position and the Sun's actual position. When the Sun was in the fast zone, they computed its future positions by using the faster velocity. When it was in the slow zone, they computed its future position by using the

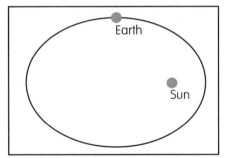

Because Earth's orbital path is an ellipse, its distance from the Sun varies. The closer the Earth is to the Sun, the faster it moves along its orbital path. The Mesopotamians detected changes in Earth's velocity but interpreted them as changes in the Sun's velocity.

slower velocity. If, during the period of interest, the Sun crossed from one zone into the other, they simply took into account the time spent in each zone. Once the zones were correctly chosen, and the speeds for each zone correctly determined, the error between what was predicted and what was observed was substantially reduced. This model, of course, is somewhat more complicated than the constant-velocity model, but it is still simple enough to use and its increase in accuracy justifies the extra work.

The Sun does not travel at one constant speed in each zone, of course. Nor does its speed suddenly change at the boundaries between the two zones. The Sun's apparent speed changes gradually all along the ecliptic. In this sense the Mesopotamian model is flawed, but it has the virtue of being useful. It enables the user to make reasonably accurate predictions of the Sun's future position.

THE TABLETS

Some of the cuneiform astronomical tablets are just tables of data or tables that show the results of computations of planetary phenomena. The actual computations are generally not included. Some tables list the times and locations of stationary points and the dates of first and last appearances of each planet for some period. The Mesopotamians were less concerned with the precise location of the planet on any particular night than with, for example, the location and time of a stationary point of the planet. These phenomena were studied almost separately from the planet itself, and the results of these observations and computations were listed in detail.

The precise methods they used to compute the tables are not so clear. The Mesopotamians did make texts, now known as Procedure Texts, that gave rules for duplicating their computations, but the Procedure Texts are very terse and difficult to interpret because they contain little detail. Ancient experts composed these tablets for other ancient experts. Not only did they not expect others to see the astronomical texts: The texts sometimes contain warnings to keep the information on the tablets secret. Modern scholars have worked hard to translate and interpret these ancient tablets. A great deal more work remains to be done. These tablets represent one of the first attempts—

The two-zone model represents one of the simplest and earliest attempts in history to employ a mathematical model to predict an astronomical phenomenon, and it worked! Furthermore mathematically speaking what can be done once can usually be done again; later the Mesopotamians divided the ecliptic into several zones, each with its own speed. This model further reduced the difference between the actual position of the Sun and its computed position. The penalty associated with this approach is that the computational work involved greatly increases. For this reason the Mesopotamians never entirely abandoned the two-zone approach, which, apparently, gave them acceptable accuracy without too much work.

The Mesopotamians approach to astronomy was built around the idea of prediction. They had little interest in developing a theory

maybe *the* first attempt—in the history of humankind to use mathematics in a systematic way to predict natural phenomena. Phenomena such as planetary stations may seem arcane to us—nowadays many well-educated people have only a hazy idea that stations exist at all. But they were important to the Mesopotamians. As an illustration of the way that the Mesopotamians kept records and as an illustration of the difficulty that scholars had in interpreting the tablets, we include a translation of a tablet relating to Jupiter:

> Jupiter on the fast arc. From disappearance to appearance, add 29 days. From appearance to the (first) stationary point, add 4 months 4 days. [From the (first)] stationary point to opposition add 58 days. From opposition to the second stationary point add 2 months 4 days. From the second stationary point to disappearance add 4 months 10 days.

(Neugebauer, Otto, ed. Astronomical Cuneiform Texts II. New York: Springer-Verlag, 1983. Page 419. Used with permission.)

As you can see, it could not be more terse. As these tablets go, however, this one is not particularly hard to understand. Many astronomical texts were more technical than this one. In Mesopotamian texts the computations and numerical data were given in base 60.

about the geometry of the solar system, a topic that would preoccupy the astronomers of ancient Greece as well as the astronomers of more recent times. Because their astronomical considerations were so different from our own, appreciating the significance of what they accomplished can be difficult. The Mesopotamians developed one of the first, perhaps *the* first, mathematical models in the history of science; they were able to use this model to predict eclipses, both lunar and solar, with moderate accuracy, and they learned to predict the motions of the Moon, Sun, and planets. All of these models are complicated by the fact that the Mesopotamians did not look below the surface. They modeled phenomena without any knowledge of the underlying *causes* of what they observed. As a consequence each phenomenon that they observed had to be analyzed separately. There is no small set of unifying concepts in Mesopotamian astronomy that allowed them to perceive all of the different phenomena they observed as somehow "the same." This absence of a theoretical framework made their system extremely complicated. At the other end of the spectrum is the approach of the Greeks. The Greeks, being more philosophically inclined, were always looking for the Big Idea, the idea that would unify their observations, and it is toward ancient Greece that we now turn our attention.

2

MATHEMATICS AND SCIENCE IN ANCIENT GREECE

While the Mesopotamians used arithmetic and a kind of proto algebra to investigate nature, the Greeks used geometry. The approach of the ancient Greeks investigating nature is, in many ways, easier to appreciate than the Mesopotamian technique. This is due, in part, to the comparative complexity of Mesopotamian methods as well as the fact that modern readers are less familiar with the goals of Mesopotamian astronomy itself. We tend to be more familiar with Greek ideas. Remember that Mesopotamian civilization was rediscovered relatively recently. By contrast Greek ideas have been a core part of Western education for many centuries. This does not imply that the Greeks were right and the Mesopotamians were wrong or backward. The two approaches were different in concept. The Mesopotamian approach was oriented to prediction. The Greek approach was often more concerned with explanation than prediction. And it would be wrong to discount style: The Greek approach impresses many readers as just plain flashier. See whether you do not agree.

Ratios and the Measure of the Universe

Greek mathematics and philosophy, according to the ancient Greeks, began with Thales of Miletus (ca. 640–ca. 546 B.C.E.). He was, according to his successors, the first of a long line of philosopher-mathematicians. During the centuries following his death his stature continued to grow among the Greeks. So much was attributed to him by later generations of philosophers—much of it without apparent justification—that knowing what his contribution actually was is difficult. Nevertheless in the stories about Thales we can find at a very elementary level much of what characterized later Greek mathematics and science. Consider the following story:

Thales, who traveled quite a bit, went to Egypt, where he learned Egyptian mathematics. As any tourist in Egypt does, Thales visited the already ancient Great Pyramid at Giza. (The Great Pyramid was well over 1,000 years old when Thales was born.) He was curious about the height of the Great Pyramid but could find no one who would (or perhaps could) tell him its height, so he decided to find out for himself. Measuring the height of the Great Pyramid directly is a tall order. The obvious problem, of course, is that it is extremely tall, but a second, more fundamental problem is its shape. By contrast if one wants to measure the height of a tall cliff, one can simply lower a rope to the base of the cliff and then measure the length of the rope required. This is impossible on a pyramid. If one lowers a rope from the apex of the pyramid to its base, one finds only the length of a side of the pyramid. The sides, however, are quite a bit longer than the pyramid is tall. In fact most of the methods a modern reader might imagine would have been mathematically difficult for Thales, or they would have been very labor-intensive. Furthermore climbing the pyramid in Thales' time would have been much more difficult than it is today because the pyramid was covered in a smooth stone sheath. Thales' solution is elegantly simple. He pushed a stick vertically into the ground in a sunny area near the pyramid. He measured the length of that part of the stick that was above the ground, and then he waited. He knew that when the length of the shadow of the stick equaled the height of the stick, the length of the shadow of the pyramid equaled the height of the pyramid. When the length of the stick's shadow equaled the stick's height, all that remained to do was to measure the length

The Great Pyramid of Giza. Thales' approach to measuring its height is still recounted thousands of years later. (Library of Congress, Prints and Photographs Division)

of the pyramid's shadow, which, since it was on the ground, was much easier to measure than the pyramid itself. By the clever use of ratios, Thales, and the many generations of Greek mathematicians who followed him, were able to make extraordinary discoveries about the universe.

Aristarchus of Samos (ca. 310–ca. 230 B.C.E.) used ratios and angles to investigate the relative distances of the Earth to the Moon and the Earth to the Sun. Aristarchus knew that each phase of the Moon is caused by the position of the Moon relative to the Earth and Sun. He knew that the reason that part of the Moon is not visible from Earth is that it is not illuminated by the Sun, and that the bright part of the Moon is bright because it is illuminated by the Sun. These simple facts enabled Aristarchus to investigate the distances from the Earth to the Moon and Earth to the Sun. To understand his method (using modern terminology) we begin by imagining three lines:

- One line connects the center of the Moon to the center of Earth

- The second line connects the center of the Moon to the center of the Sun

- The third line connects the center of the Sun to the center of Earth

In this particular essay Aristarchus used the idea that both the Moon and the Sun revolve around Earth. As they revolve around Earth, the lines connecting the centers of the three bodies form a triangle that continually changes shape. When the Moon is exactly half-illuminated, the triangle formed by the three bodies has to be a right triangle. (The Moon would be situated at the vertex of the right angle.) Next he tried to measure the angle that had Earth as its vertex (see the diagram). He estimated this angle at 87°. Because he knew that (in modern terminology) the sum of the interior angles of a triangle is always 180°, he concluded that the last angle, the angle with vertex at the Sun, measured 3° (3° + 87° + 90° = 180°).

Now he knew the *shape* of the triangle formed when the Moon was half illuminated, but this knowledge is not quite enough information to find the absolute distances between the three bodies. (One can know the shape of a triangle without knowing its size.) Nevertheless Aristarchus had enough information to estimate the *ratios of their distances.* He concluded that the Earth-Sun distance is 18 to 20 times greater than the Earth-Moon distance. (This ratio holds for the corresponding sides of any right triangle con-

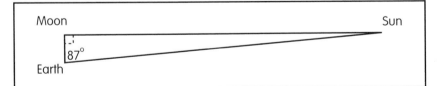

Aristarchus computed the distance from Earth to the Sun in multiples of the Earth-Moon distance by studying the triangle with vertices at the Moon, Earth, and Sun.

taining an 87° angle.) Today we know that the Sun is actually about 370 times farther from Earth than is the Moon, but this does not indicate a fault in Aristarchus's thinking. In fact his method is flawless. His only mistake was in *measuring the angle* whose vertex was located at Earth. The angle is not 87°—it is more like 89° 50'.

In addition to finding a method to estimate the ratios of the distances between the Earth, Sun, and Moon, Aristarchus used similar geometric methods to estimate the *ratios of the sizes* of the three bodies. Once again his method is sound, but his measurements are not especially accurate. Notice that here, too, Aristarchus is able to estimate only the

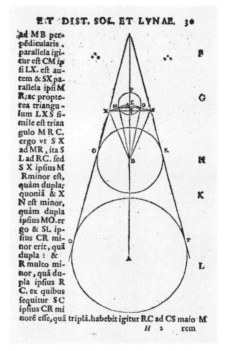

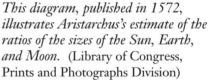

This diagram, published in 1572, illustrates Aristarchus's estimate of the ratios of the sizes of the Sun, Earth, and Moon. (Library of Congress, Prints and Photographs Division)

relative sizes of the Earth, Moon, and Sun. He does not have enough information to estimate their absolute sizes, but if he had known the diameter of one of the three bodies, he could have used this information to compute the diameters of the other two. He was very close to solving the entire problem. Interestingly Archimedes of Syracuse, one of the most successful mathematicians of all time, gave credit to Aristarchus for advocating (in another work) the idea that Earth orbits the Sun. Unfortunately Aristarchus's writings on this subject have been lost.

Eratosthenes of Cyrene (276–194 B.C.E.) found a way to measure the circumference of Earth. Eratosthenes was a mathematician and librarian at the great library at Alexandria, Egypt. His method of finding Earth's circumference is a somewhat more sophisticated version of Thales's method for finding the height of the Great Pyramid. To estimate the circumference of Earth, Eratosthenes made two assumptions. First, he assumed that Earth is a sphere. Second, he assumed that the rays of the Sun are parallel with each other. Along with these assumptions he made use of a fact about a deep well that had been dug in the town of Syene. Syene was located directly south of Alexandria.

Eratosthenes knew that on a certain day of the year at a certain time of the day the Sun shone directly into the well at Syene. This well was deep and it was dug straight into the Earth, so Eratosthenes knew that on that day at that time one could draw a line from the center of the Earth through the well right to the center of the Sun. On the day (and at the time) that the Sun shone directly into the well at Syene, Eratosthenes placed a stick in the ground at Alexandria and measured the length of the shadow cast by the stick. If the stick had been in Syene it would not have cast any shadow at all, because it would have pointed directly at the Sun. At Alexandria, however, the stick cast a very clear and definite shadow. Eratosthenes' reasoning, expressed in modern notation, is described in the following. Refer, also, to the accompanying figure.

- Eratosthenes imagines extending the ray of light that passes through the center of the well straight down to the center of Earth. Call this line l_1.

- He imagines extending the line determined by the stick straight down to the center of Earth. Call this line l_2. Every line that is perpendicular to Earth's surface points at Earth's center so l_1 and l_2 intersect at Earth's center.

- There is a third line to take into account. This is the line determined by the ray of sunlight that strikes the end of the stick. Call this line l_3. Because Eratosthenes assumed that rays of light from the Sun are parallel, l_1 and l_3 are parallel, and l_2, the line determined by the stick, forms two equal acute (less than 90°) angles, where it crosses l_1 and l_3.

- Of course Eratosthenes could not see the angle formed at Earth's center, but he knew how to use the height of the stick and the length of the shadow cast by the stick to *compute* the angle formed at the tip of the stick by the Sun's ray, l_3, and the stick itself, l_2. This angle equals the angle at Earth's center.

- Because Earth is spherical, the *ratio* formed by the angle at Earth's center to 360° is equal to the ratio formed by the distance from Alexandria to Syene to the distance all the way around the planet.

Eratosthenes knew the distance from Syene to Alexandria. He had measured the angle that the Sun's rays made with the vertical stick at Alexandria. This, in modern terminology, is the equation that he used to find Earth's circumference:

(Angle at Alexandria)/360 = (distance from Syene to Alexandria)/(circumference of Earth)

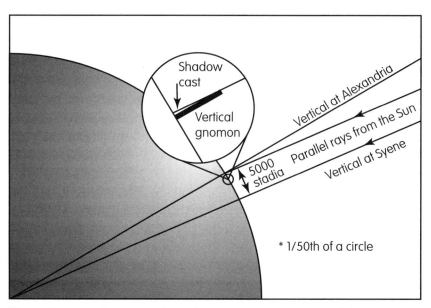

Eratosthenes used ratios and simple measurements to successfully compute the circumference of the Earth.

Because he knew everything except the circumference of Earth, he was able to solve the equation and in so doing *compute* the circumference of Earth. This method of computing the circumference of our planet can yield good results and is a popular student project even today. Eratosthenes' own estimate of Earth's circumference was within about 20 percent of the modern value.

The geometrical methods used by Eratosthenes and Aristarchus to investigate the universe were characteristic of Greek science. These methods give very good results provided the assumptions are correct and the measurements are accurate. Notice, too, that there is no concept of energy, force, or mass in Eratosthenes' or Aristarchus's method. This, too, is characteristic of most of Greek science. The Greek philosopher Aristotle described what it is that mathematicians study:

> But, as the mathematician speculates from abstraction (for he contemplates by abstracting all sensible natures, as, for instance, gravity and levity, hardness and its contrary, and besides these, heat and cold, and other sensible contrarieties), but alone leaves quantity and the continuous, of which some pertain to one, others to two, and others to three [dimensions].
>
> *(Aristotle.* The Metaphysics of Aristotle, *translated by Thomas Taylor. London: Davis, Wilks, and Taylor, Chancery-Lane, 1801.)*

In our time there are mathematical theories that incorporate the concepts of "gravity" (weight), levity (lightness), hardness, and "heat and cold" (temperature), and that sometimes extend to more dimensions than three, but during the time of Aristotle, for the most part mathematicians investigated only geometric phenomena. Their methods, their conclusions, and their choice of phenomena to study all reflect this emphasis on geometrical thinking.

A Geometry of the Universe

One of the last and perhaps the most famous of all Greek astronomers is Claudius Ptolemy. Although we do not know the dates of his birth and death, we do know that he was busy making observations from C.E. 121 until C.E. 151. In addition to his work in astronomy and mathematics, Ptolemy wrote books on geography and optics that were well received in his time. Ptolemy's main work, which is about mathematics and astronomy, is called the *Almagest.* It contains many theorems about trigonometry but is best remembered because it describes a geometric model of the visible universe. Ptolemy wanted to explain the motions of the stars and the planets, the Moon, and the Sun, and to this end he wrote much of the *Almagest.* The ideas expressed in this book did not, for the most part, begin with Ptolemy, but it was in his book that these ideas found their greatest expression. Ptolemy's ideas on the geometry of the universe influenced astronomers for well over 1,000 years. In addition to Greek astronomers, Ptolemy's ideas influenced generations of Islamic and European astronomers.

We can find much of the inspiration for Ptolemy's ideas in the work of Eudoxus of Cnidas (408–355 B.C.E.). Eudoxus was one of the great mathematicians of his day. In order to explain the motions of the stars and planets Eudoxus imagined that the heavens are spherical—the standard name for this model is a celestial sphere—and that a spherical Earth is located at the center of the spherical heavens. Eudoxus imagined that the diameter of Earth is very small compared to the diameter of the celestial sphere, and he attributed the motions of the stars to the fact that the celestial sphere rotates about Earth once each day. None of Eudoxus's works has survived; we know of him because he is quoted in the works of many later Greek writers. The idea that the heavens are spherical and that the motions of the heavens can be explained by the rotation of one or more spheres is extremely important in Greek thinking. If one accepts these ideas about the shape of the universe, one can prove in a mathematical way various consequences of this "heavenly geometry." What Eudoxus's model could not do, however, was account for the observed motions of the Sun, Moon, and planets across the sky.

In the third century B.C.E. Apollonius of Perga (ca. 262–ca. 190 B.C.E.), one of the most prominent of all Greek mathematicians, proposed a new model, a major refinement of Eudoxus's ideas.

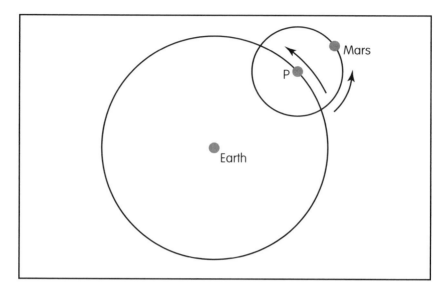

Apollonius's model for the motion of Mars. Apollonius attempted to account for the retrograde motion of planets by imagining one circular motion imposed on another.

Apollonius's goal was to provide a model that accounted for retrograde planetary motion. (See the discussion of retrograde motion in the section on Mesopotamian astronomy in chapter 1.) Apollonius imagined a planet—Jupiter, for example—moving in a small circle, while the center of the small circle moved in a large circle centered on Earth. (Notice that Apollonius used circles rather than spheres.) When the planet's motion along the small circle is in the same general direction as the small circle's motion along the large circle, the planet, *when viewed from Earth*, appears to move forward (see the accompanying diagram). When the planet's motion along the small circle is in the direction opposite that of the small circle's motion along the large circle, and if the relative speeds of motion along the two circles are in the "right" ratio, the planet's motion, when viewed from Earth, appears backward or retrograde.

This is a complicated model and in Ptolemy's hands it became even more complicated. Most ancient Greek astronomers preferred to imagine that all the planets move along circular paths at constant speed. There was no "scientific" reason for this belief. It was a philosophical preference, but it was a preference that persisted in one form or another throughout the history of Greek astronomy. As more data on the actual motion of the Sun, Moon, and planets were acquired, however, Apollonius's complicated model proved to be not complicated enough to account for the observed motions of the planets.

Another important influence on Ptolemy was Hipparchus (ca. 190–ca. 120 B.C.E.). Hipparchus contributed a number of important observations and computations to Greek astronomy, among them the observation that the seasons are of different lengths. (The seasons are defined astronomically. For example, the beginning of spring and the beginning of autumn occur when the Sun is so positioned that a straight line connecting the center of Earth with the center of the Sun passes through the equator. This happens twice a year, at the vernal equinox and the autumnal equinox.) Hipparchus recognized that because the seasons have different lengths, the speed of the Sun along the ecliptic—the ecliptic is the name of the apparent path traveled by the Sun across the sky—cannot be constant. As we have already mentioned, the Mesopotamians had already made the observation that the Sun's apparent speed is not constant. Apparently Hipparchus's discovery was made independently of the Mesopotamians'. In any case the Greek solution to the complicated motions of the heavens was not to abandon the idea of a celestial sphere but to imagine an even more complicated structure.

All of these ideas and difficulties culminated in the *Almagest* and in a short separate book, *Planetary Hypotheses*. In the *Almagest* Ptolemy takes great pains to make his system accurate in the sense that it explains the motions actually observed. He also works to make his system orderly and logically coherent. He prefers to think of the small circles of Apollonius as the equators of small spheres. By arranging multiple spheres one inside the other and allowing them to revolve at different rates and on different axes, and by placing Earth in the right place inside all of this spherical motion, Ptolemy produces a mechanical model that reproduces (more or less) the complicated series of motions of the Sun, Moon, planets, and stars that the Greeks had now measured and documented. The agreement was not perfect, but it was better than that of earlier Greek models.

Ptolemy's mechanical model of the universe is clever and entertaining geometry. He accounts for the motions of the universe with a complicated and invisible system of interlocking spheres that rotate within and without and about one another as gears do in a particularly complicated clock. There is no physics in the *Almagest*—at least not in a modern sense. It does not explore the concepts of mass or force or energy; rather it explains facts about stellar and planetary motions that were already established. Insofar as records about past events are useful for predicting future events, Ptolemy's model is useful for predicting future motions. It cannot be used to uncover new phenomena or new celestial objects.

Nevertheless, the effect of the *Almagest* on Western thought was profound. The ideas expressed in Ptolemy's books were accepted for about 14 centuries; one could argue that the *Almagest* is one of the most influential books ever written. We might wonder how anyone could have accepted these ideas. To be fair, there are elements that can be found in the *Almagest* itself that contributed to its longevity as a "scientific" document. As previously mentioned, for example, by the time Ptolemy had finished tinkering with the motions of all of his spheres, his system did account for the movements of the stars, Moon, Sun, and planets with reasonable accuracy.

Another reason was that many later generations of philosophers held the Greeks in such high regard that they were reluctant to criticize the conclusions of the major Greek thinkers, Ptolemy included. (This reluctance to criticize major Greek thinkers was a reluctance that the ancient Greeks themselves did not share.) Many European philosophers went even further: They believed that the Greeks had already learned most of what could be learned. They believed that later generations were obliged to acquaint themselves with the work of "the ancients" and to refine the ancient teachings where that was possible. They did not believe that one should make major revisions of Greek thought. This attitude was a serious barrier to progress for a very long time.

A ROTATING EARTH

Ptolemy was aware that there were others who argued that the sky does not rotate. They believed that the best explanation for the motion of the stars is a rotating Earth. From our perspective it seems obvious that it is the Earth and not the sky that rotates, but Ptolemy presents some fairly persuasive arguments for the impossibility of a rotating Earth. Before we dismiss the work of Ptolemy we should ask ourselves how many of his arguments against a rotating Earth we can refute from our vantage point almost 2,000 years into Ptolemy's future. Here, taken from Ptolemy's own writings, are some of the reasons that he believes that the Earth cannot rotate. (As you read this excerpt, keep in mind that someone standing on Earth's equator is traveling around Earth's axis of rotation at about 1,000 miles per hour (1,600 kph).

> as far as appearances of the stars are concerned, nothing would perhaps keep things from being in accordance with this simpler conjecture [that the Earth revolves on its axis], but in light of what happens around us in the air such a notion would seem altogether absurd . . . they [those who support the idea of a rotating Earth] would have to admit that the earth's turning is the swiftest of absolutely all the movements about it because of its making so great a revolution in a short time, so that all those things that were not at rest on the earth would seem to have a movement contrary to it, and never would a cloud be seen to move toward the east nor anything else that flew or was thrown into the air. For the earth would always outstrip them in its eastward motion, so that all other bodies would seem to be left behind and to move towards the west.
>
> For if they should say that the air is also carried around with the earth in the same direction and at the same speed, none the less the bodies contained in it would always seem to be outstripped by the movement of both. Or if they should be carried around as if one with the air, . . . these bodies would always remain in the same relative position and there would be no movement or change either in the case of flying bodies or projectiles. And yet we shall clearly see all such things taking place as if their slowness or swiftness did not follow at all from the earth's movement.

(Ptolemy. Almagest. Translated by Catesby Taliafero. Great Books of the Western World. Chicago: Encyclopaedia Britannica, 1952.

As late as the 17th century Galileo was, on peril of death, fighting for the right to investigate and refute the ancient teachings. This closed-mindedness, of course, was unrelated to Ptolemy. Ptolemy was simply trying to describe the universe as it appeared to him.

Archimedes: Fusing Physics with Mathematics

In our story Archimedes of Syracuse (ca. 287–212 B.C.E.) occupies a special place. He considered himself a mathematician—in fact, he wanted his tombstone to illustrate his favorite geometrical theorem—and he certainly has an important role in that long tradition of outstanding Greek mathematicians. But his discoveries extend beyond mathematics. He studied force and density, aspects of what we would now call physics, and he found ways to use his discoveries to solve important practical problems. Significantly he did more than study physics: He used rigorous mathematical methods to obtain solutions to physics problems. In fact he *deduced* additional physical properties from a small number of initial physical assumptions in the same way that a mathematician proves additional properties of a mathematical system by using logic and a small number of axioms and definitions. This union of mathematics and physics became a hallmark of the work of Simon Stevin, Galileo Galilei, and other scientists of the Renaissance; it is one of the most lasting contributions of Renaissance scientists to contemporary science. But the Renaissance did not begin until about 1,600 years after Archimedes' death, so it is no exaggeration to say that for more than 16 centuries Archimedes' work set the standard for excellence in research in the physical sciences.

A mathematical approach to the study of physics is important because today natural laws are generally formulated mathematically. It is often possible to deduce previously undiscovered properties of physical systems by studying the mathematical consequences of the laws themselves as well as the mathematical consequences of previous discoveries. Many scientists who lecture on topics ranging from rocket science to population genetics begin their seminars by outlining the *governing equations:* These are the mathematical statements that describe the basic properties of the

44 ΑΡΧΙΜΗΔΟΥΣ

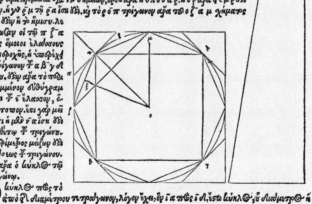

ΑΡΧΙΜΗΔΟΥΣ ΚΥ
ΚΛΟΥ ΜΕΤΡΗΣΙΣ.

This page of Archimedes' work, written in Greek and showing inscribed and circumscribed figures, was published in 1544. (Library of Congress, Prints and Photographs Division)

systems that they study. This mathematical approach is now fundamental to our understanding of what science is, and in the ancient world Archimedes' work is the best example of this approach. Two cases that illustrate Archimedes' ability to express physical problems in mathematical language are his works on buoyancy and levers. A third discovery by Archimedes, an estimate of the number π, is important to our story because of the method of his discovery and not the facts that he uncovered.

Archimedes wrote two volumes on the phenomenon of buoyancy, *On Floating Bodies, I and II.* This work is largely written as a sequence of statements about objects in fluids. Each statement is accompanied by mathematical proof of its correctness. Archimedes' most famous discovery about fluids is now known as Archimedes' principle of buoyancy. The goal of the buoyancy principle is to describe a *force*, the force that we call the buoyancy force. The buoyancy force is directed upward. It opposes the weight of an object, which is a downward-directed force. All objects near Earth's surface have weight; only objects that are wholly or partially immersed in a fluid are subject to the buoyancy force. Ships, for example, whether made of wood as in Archimedes' time or steel as in our own time, are kept afloat by the buoyancy force.

But the buoyancy force does more than float boats. When an object does not float—for example, when it sinks beneath the surface—it is still subject to the buoyancy force; in this case the buoyancy force is simply not strong enough to prevent the object from sinking. It is, however, strong enough to support part of the weight of the object. In fact if we weigh the object underwater, our scale will show that the object's underwater weight is less than its weight on dry land. The difference between the two weights is (approximately) the strength of the buoyancy force on that object. In some general way this is known to everyone who works near the water. Salvage operators—and there have been salvage operators for as long as there have been ships—know from experience that it is easier to lift an object that is underwater than it is to lift that same object after it breaks the water's surface. Archimedes, however, knew more. Archimedes discovered that the strength of the buoyancy force *equals* the weight of the mass of water displaced by the object.

In *On Floating Bodies* Archimedes breaks the buoyancy force into two cases. In one case he discusses what happens when the solid is denser than the surrounding fluid. He describes this situation by saying the solid is "heavier than a fluid." In the other case he discusses what happens when the solid is less dense than the surrounding fluid. He describes this situation by saying the solid is "lighter than a fluid." Here is the buoyancy principle expressed in Archimedes' own words:

- A solid heavier than a fluid will, if placed in it, descend to the bottom of the fluid, and the solid will, when weighed in the fluid, be lighter than its true weight by the weight of the fluid displaced.

- Any solid lighter than a fluid will, if placed in the fluid, be so far immersed that the weight of the solid will be equal to the weight of the fluid displaced.

> (*Archimedes.* On Floating Bodies, I and II. *Translated by Sir Thomas L. Heath.* Great Books of the Western World, *Vol. 11. Chicago: Encyclopaedia Britannica, 1952.)*

Archimedes' principle establishes a link between a geometric property and a force. If we know the volume of an object—that is, the geometric property—then we can *predict* the upward force a fluid exerts on the object when the object is completely immersed: The upward force equals the weight of a body of fluid whose volume equals the volume of the object itself.

Archimedes expended a great deal of effort investigating how these ideas applied to specific geometric forms; he was fascinated with both the physics and the geometry involved. But it is the general principle and the way it links forces and geometry that are important to us.

Today we have a much broader understanding of the word *fluid* than Archimedes did. Scientists now use the word *fluid* to refer to both liquids and gases—in fact, anything that flows is now classified as a fluid—and we now know that Archimedes' principle applies to any fluid. Archimedes is often described as the founder of the science of fluids, and there is to this day no introductory text on the science of fluids that does not begin with some version of Archimedes' principle of buoyancy. His work marks the beginning of one of the oldest, most useful, and most mathematically challenging branches of science, the science of fluids, a subject about which we have much to say later.

The Law of the Lever

In addition to the principle of buoyancy, Archimedes established what is now called the law of the lever. Archimedes was not the first person to use a lever, of course. People all over the planet had been using levers long before the birth of Archimedes, and they must have known the general principle of the lever. It is simple enough: The farther from the fulcrum one pushes, the greater the force one exerts. In fact even the mathematical expression of this idea was known before Archimedes. The philosopher Aristotle wrote about levers before Archimedes, and Aristotle's writings indicate that he understood the general mathematical principles involved. Despite all of this Archimedes is still often described as the discoverer of the law of the lever, and that is correct, too. Sometimes in the history of an idea what one knows is less important than how one knows it. Archimedes' work on levers is a beautiful example of this. He demonstrates how one can use rigorous mathematics to investigate nature.

The law of the lever can be found in Archimedes' two-volume treatise *On the Equilibrium of Planes,* a remarkable scientific work. In *On the Equilibrium of Planes* Archimedes adopts the method found in the most famous mathematics book from antiquity, the *Elements* by Euclid of Alexandria. That is, he begins his book by

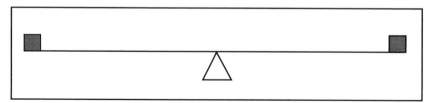

"Equal weights at equal distances are in equilibrium" (Archimedes)

listing the *postulates*, the statements that he later uses to deduce his conclusions. The seven postulates describe the fundamental properties of bodies in equilibrium. This, for example, is how Archimedes states his first postulate:

> Equal weights at equal distances [*from the fulcrum*] are in equilibrium, and equal weights at unequal distances are not in equilibrium but incline towards the weight which is at the greater distance.

> > (*Archimedes*. On the Equilibrium of Planes or The Centers of Gravity of Planes, Book I. *Translated by Sir Thomas Heath*. Great Books of the Western World. *Vol. 11. Chicago: Encyclopaedia Britannica, 1952.*)

This and the remaining six postulates describe the mathematical system that Archimedes plans to investigate. After listing the postulates, he immediately begins to state and prove ideas that are the logical consequences of the postulates. Each statement is accompanied by a proof that demonstrates how the statement is related to the postulates. These statements and proofs correspond to the theorems and proofs in Euclid's *Elements*. In Archimedes's hands levers are transformed into a purely mathematical problem.

Notice that in Archimedes' first postulate, which is quoted in the previous paragraph, the idea of symmetry is very important. "Equal weights at equal distances" is a very symmetric arrangement. He uses the idea of symmetry to connect the idea of weight, which is a force, and distance, which is a geometric property. Each postulate describes some aspect of the relation between weights and distances. Mathematically speaking, once Archimedes has listed his postulates, all that is left is to deduce some of the consequences of these ideas. His approach is a compelling one: If you accept his assumptions (postulates), then you must also accept his conclusions.

As Archimedes develops his ideas, he shows that it is possible to disturb the symmetry of an arrangement of weights in different ways and still maintain a balance, or *equilibrium*. In a step-by-step manner he derives the basic (mathematical) properties of the lever. It is a remarkable intellectual achievement and a beautiful example of what we now call mathematical physics: The postulates describe the connection between a natural phenomenon and his mathematical model, and the theorems describe the logical connections that exist between the postulates. *On the Equilibrium of Planes* is a stunning example of the way mathematics can be used to model natural phenomena.

Archimedes' *Measurement of a Circle*

The last of Archimedes' contributions that we consider here concerns his estimate of the number π. The symbol π is the Greek letter pi (pronounced "pie"). It represents a number whose approximate

THE SIEGE OF SYRACUSE

During his long life Archimedes made an enormous impression on friend and foe alike through his work with levers and other simple machines. During peacetime Archimedes had demonstrated his understanding of simple machines by moving a ship along a beach. The ship was a three-masted merchant ship that had been pulled up on the beach by a large group of men. Archimedes had the ship loaded with cargo and men and attached one of his devices to the boat; then with the help of his device he pulled the ship along the beach by himself.

Later when Archimedes was elderly, the Romans attacked the Greek city-state of Syracuse. Archimedes worked hard to defend his nation against the invaders. Syracuse was located by the sea and could be attacked by both land and water. Archimedes used his discoveries about simple machines such as levers and pulleys to devise new types of weapons to defend Syracuse against the Roman army and navy. These weapons included new types of catapults to prevent the Romans from attacking by land and new types of cranes to prevent the Roman ships from attacking the sea wall of Syracuse. These weapons were very effective. Under the direction of the general Marcellus the Romans eventually ceased to attack and, instead, surrounded the city and waited. This siege continued for two years. Eventually, however, the people of Syracuse were defeated by the Romans, and Archimedes was killed by a Roman soldier not long after the city was occupied. This is part of an value is 3.1415. (The number π is very important because it is critical in many branches of mathematics.)

Archimedes' approach to estimating the size of π is an application of an idea called the method of exhaustion. Eudoxus of Cnidas is credited with discovering the idea. Archimedes' approach to employing the method of exhaustion, however, is original. To understand Archimedes' idea knowing a little about π is helpful.

The number π can be represented as a ratio. If we divide the circumference of a circle by its diameter, the result is π. This is true for every circle: If we multiply the diameter by π we get the circumference. Over the centuries mathematicians have discovered many peculiar properties of the number π, but all of these

account of the siege written by the Roman historian Plutarch (ca. C.E. 46–ca. C.E. 120):

> When, therefore, the Romans assaulted them by sea and land, the Syracusans were stricken dumb with terror; they thought that nothing could withstand so furious an onset by such forces. But Archimedes began to ply his engines, and shot against the land forces of the assailants all sorts of missiles and immense masses of stones, which came down with incredible din and speed; nothing whatever could ward off their weight, but they knocked down in heaps those who stood in their way, and threw their ranks into confusion. At the same time huge beams were suddenly projected over the ships from the walls, which sank some of them with great weights plunging down from on high; others were seized by the prow by iron claws, or beaks like the beaks of cranes, drawn straight up into the air, and then plunged stern foremost into the depths, or were turned round and round by means of enginery within the city, and dashed upon the steep cliffs that jutted out beneath the wall of the city, with great destruction of the fighting men on board, . . . so that Marcellus, in perplexity, ordered his ships to sail back as fast as they could, and his land forces to retire.

(Plutarch. Plutarch's Lives. *Translated by Bernadotte Perrin. New York: Macmillan, 1917)*

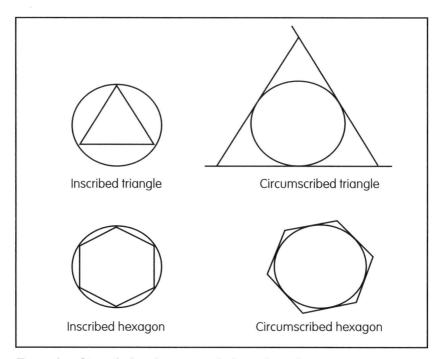

Inscribed triangle   Circumscribed triangle

Inscribed hexagon   Circumscribed hexagon

Examples of inscribed and circumscribed regular polygons

properties were unknown to Archimedes. His question was more elementary. He wanted to know exactly how big π is. This simple question has no obvious connection to the laws of nature, but Archimedes' approach to answering this "simple" question can be employed to solve many important scientific problems.

Because π is defined as the ratio of the circumference of a circle to its diameter, finding π can be reduced to finding the circumference of a circle whose diameter is equal to 1. (When the diameter of a circle is 1, the circumference of a circle divided by the diameter is still the circumference.)

Archimedes does not try to find π directly; that is too hard. Instead, he tried to approximate π and, as any good mathematician would, attempted to find the size of the error in his approximation. To do this he locates two numbers, one slightly larger than π and the other slightly smaller than π. Archimedes' paper describing how he approximates π, *Measurement of a Circle*, is one of the most famous papers in the history of mathematics.

Archimedes chooses a roundabout method because he has no way of directly measuring the length of a circular arc. Instead he approximates the circle with polygons. Polygons are plane figures with straight sides, and as a circle does, they enclose a region of the plane. Unlike the perimeter of a circle the perimeter of a polygon is relatively easy to calculate. Archimedes finds the circumference of the polygons rather than the circumference of the circle. In fact he makes his work even easier by using regular polygons. The sides of a regular polygon are all of equal length, so all he has to do to find the circumference of a regular polygon is find the length of one of its sides and then multiply that length by the number of sides. The more closely the shape of the polygon approximates a circular shape, the more closely its circumference approximates the circumference of the circle. To find the size of his error in approximating the circumference, he deliberately uses one polygon whose circumference is too small and one whose circumference is too large.

We can demonstrate Archimedes' method with equilateral triangles. (Equilateral triangles are the simplest of regular polygons.) The triangle that lies entirely inside the circle is called an inscribed triangle. It is the largest equilateral triangle that can fit inside the circle. Notice that its circumference is smaller than that of the circle. The triangle that lies outside the circle is called a circumscribed triangle. It is the smallest equilateral triangle that can enclose the circle, and its circumference is larger than that of the circle. If we let a lowercase *c* represent the smaller circumference and a capital *C* represent the larger circumference, then we can summarize Archimedes' result with the following symbols:

$$c < \pi < C$$

Triangles are, however, poor approximations to circles. To do better we could use hexagons (see the figure). The circumference of the inscribed hexagon is smaller than that of the circle and larger than that of an inscribed triangle. The circumference of the circumscribed hexagon is larger than that of the circle but smaller than that of a circumscribed triangle. Archimedes uses regular polygons with 96 sides. He concludes that

$$3\ 10/71 < \pi < 3\ 10/70$$

That is a pretty good estimate, but there were other estimates in other ancient cultures as good or better. What is important for our story is not the result but the method. Archimedes finds a way to develop an approximation that has two very important properties: (1) The method can always be extended indefinitely to obtain ever more accurate approximations (in this case that means using regular polygons with more sides) and (2) a rigorous bound for the error is always produced, so that we not only know that we have a "good" approximation, but also know how good an approximation it is. Later in this volume we will see how Archimedes' method was modified and extended by other scientists to study a variety of physical phenomena. In fact this method contains the beginnings of the field of mathematics that we now call calculus.

Much of Greek science was simply applied geometry. Philosophically the Greeks were inclined to search for unifying ideas, but as a matter of practice, they concentrated on describing the size and shape of things without much regard to underlying principles such as force and mass. With respect to their geometric investigations, however, they were very successful. This was a culture with an extremely simple technology, whose mathematicians computed, among other things, the circumference of Earth and the relative distances of the Earth to the Moon and the Earth to the Sun. Impressive as Greek science is, Archimedes stands in a class by himself. Alone among Greek scientists he successfully seeks to identify underlying causes. His investigations into the relationships between geometry and forces, as exemplified by his works on buoyancy and levers, were not surpassed for more than 1,000 years.

Finally, it should be noted that our assessment of Archimedes' importance is a modern one. It was not shared by the many generations of Persian, Arabic, and European scholars who studied, debated, and absorbed the works of the ancient Greeks during the first 16 or 17 centuries following Archimedes' death. They studied Archimedes' work, of course, but other Greek scientists and mathematicians were more thoroughly studied and quoted than Archimedes. The works of Ptolemy, for example, now recognized as simply incorrect, and the work of Euclid of Alexandria (fl. 300 B.C.E.), now acknowledged as much more elementary than that of Archimedes, exerted a far greater influence on the history of science and mathematics than anything that Archimedes wrote. One reason is that Archimedes' writing style is generally harder to read than the writings of many of his contemporaries. It is terser; he generally provides less in the way of supporting work. Archimedes requires more from the reader even when he is solving a simple problem. But it is more than a matter of style. The problems that he solves are generally harder than those of most of his contemporaries. Archimedes solved problems that were commensurate with his exceptional abilities. But one last reason that Archimedes had less influence on the history of science and mathematics than many of his contemporaries is simply the result of bad luck. His writings were simply less available. The most astonishing example of this concerns his book *The Method*. Archimedes had an unusual and productive way of looking at problems. He was aware of this, and he wanted to communicate this method of investigating mathematics and nature to his contemporaries in the hope that they would benefit. The result was a book called *The Method*. It is in *The Method* that Archimedes describes the very concrete, physical way that he investigated problems. He wrote this book so that others might benefit from his experience and discover new facts and ideas themselves. In *The Method*, the interested reader can learn a little more of how one of history's greatest thinkers thought. Unfortunately, *The Method* was lost early on. It was rediscovered early in the 20th century in a library in what is now Istanbul, Turkey, far too late to influence the course of mathematical or scientific investigation.

3

A PERIOD OF TRANSITION

The mathematically oriented sciences of antiquity developed large-ly without reference to the fundamental concepts of mass, force, and energy. We have seen that this was true of the Mesopotamians and the Greeks (except Archimedes), and the situation was the same in other early mathematically advanced cultures. The Indians, the Chinese, and the Arabs also had strong traditions in astronomy, for example, but they were also interested in geometrical measure-ments and predictions. The geometrical aspects of astronomy fas-cinated them, but they showed little interest in uncovering the causes of the motions that they so carefully documented. In many ways and for a very long time science *was* applied geometry. In Europe during the late Middle Ages a period of transition of sev-eral hundred years began as mathematicians and scientists aban-doned the old ideas in the search for deeper insights into the physical world.

Progress was slow. It took time to identify a reasonable rela-tionship between theory and experiment. The fondness that the Greeks showed for theory over experiment also thoroughly per-vaded European thinking throughout the Middle Ages. Scholars spent a great deal of time debating the ideas of "the ancients." This, in fact, was their principal focus. They spent much less time examining nature as it existed around them. On the author-ity of their ancient Greek predecessors they felt justified dis-missing what experimental evidence did exist whenever it conflicted with their own preconceived notions of what was true and what was false. Nor was this the only barrier to progress. The ideas of conservation of mass, momentum, and energy evolved slowly, because they depended on a deeper and very different understanding of nature than did the geometric ideas that had for so long prevailed. Finally, the mathematics necessary to express what we now regard as the basic laws of nature had, for the most part, not been developed. Without the necessary mathematics there was simply too much speculation. Without mathematics there was not a mutually agreed upon, unambiguous language available in which they could express their ideas. Without mathematics it was much harder to separate useful ideas from useless ones.

Nicholas Oresme

In the 14th century ideas about mathematics and the physical sciences began to change. Nowhere is this better illustrated than in the work of Nicholas Oresme (ca. 1325–82), a French mathematician, economist, and clergyman. As a young man Oresme studied theology in Paris. He spent his adult life serving in the Roman Catholic Church. His life of service required him to move from place to place. Many of the moves he made involved accepting positions of increased authority. In addition to fulfilling his religious responsibilities, Oresme exerted a lot of secular authority, due, in part, to a well-placed friend. As a young man Oresme had developed a friendship with the heir to the throne of France, the future King Charles V.

Aristotle, Ptolemy, and Copernicus discussing astronomy. Published in 1632 (Library of Congress, Prints and Photographs Division)

Oresme was remarkably forward-thinking. He argued against astrology and even provided a clever mathematical reason that astrology is not dependable. It is a tenet of astrology that the motions of the heavens are cyclic. Oresme argued that the allegedly cyclic relationships studied by the astrologers are not cyclic at all. Cyclic relationships can be represented by rational numbers, that is, the quotient of two whole numbers. Oresme argued that the motions of the heavens are, instead, incommensurable with one another—another way of saying that they are more accurately represented by using irrational numbers. If one accepted his premise, then truly cyclic motions could not occur.

Oresme's most famous contribution is a graphical analysis of motion under constant acceleration or deceleration. Today his approach, which involves graphing a function, is familiar to students the world over, but Oresme appears to have been the first person to put together all the necessary concepts. He begins with two perpendicular lines that he calls the latitude and the longitude. These are what we now call the x-axis and the y-axis. The points along the latitude, or x-axis, represent successive instants of time. Points along the longitude, or y-axis, represent different velocities: the greater the longitude, the greater the velocity. To see how this works, suppose that an object moves for a period at constant velocity. Because the velocity is constant, the motion can be represented by a line parallel to the latitude, or x-axis. The length of the line represents the amount of time the object is in motion. If we imagine this horizontal line as the upper edge of a rectangle—the lower edge is the corresponding part of the latitude—then the distance the object travels is just the area of the rectangle. Another way of expressing the same idea is that the distance traveled is the area beneath the velocity line.

Now suppose that the velocity of the object steadily decreases until the object comes to a stop. This situation can be represented by a diagonal line that terminates on the latitude, or x-axis. The steeper the line, the faster the object stops. We can think of this diagonal line as the hypotenuse of a right triangle (see the accompanying diagram). Now suppose that we draw a line parallel to the latitude that also passes through the midpoint of the hypotenuse of the triangle. We can use this line to form a rectangle with the same base as the triangle and *with the same area* as the triangle. Oresme reasoned that the distance traveled by the object under constant deceleration equals the area below the diagonal line. The area below the diagonal line is also equal to the area below the horizontal line, but the area below the horizontal line is the average of the initial and

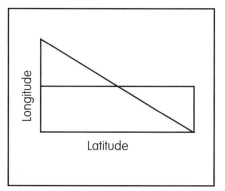

Oresme's graphical analysis of motion at constant deceleration

final velocities. His conclusion? When an object moves under constant deceleration, the distance traveled equals the average of the initial and final velocities multiplied by the amount of time spent in transit. (The case of constant acceleration can be taken into account by reversing the direction of the sloping line so that it points upward to the right instead of downward.) It is a clever interpretation of his graph, although geometrically all that he has done is find the area beneath the diagonal line.

The importance of Oresme's representation of motion lies, in part, in the fact that it *is* a representation of motion. It is a graphical representation of velocity as a function of time, and Oresme's new mathematical idea—the graphing of a function—solves an important physics problem. Even today if we relabel the latitude as the *x*-axis and the longitude as the *y*-axis, we have a very useful example of graphical analysis. To see the value of Oresme's insight, try to imagine the solution without the graph; it is a much harder problem. This highly creative and useful approach to problem solving predates similar, albeit more advanced work by Galileo by about two centuries.

Oresme's other important innovation is his treatment of infinite series. This idea was new to Western thought. The Greeks were aware of the existence of infinite sets, of course. Euclid, for example, in his work *Elements* proved that the set of prime numbers contains infinitely many elements, but in general the Greeks avoided infinite sets. Infinite sets have a number of properties that do not conform to our intuition. The Greeks largely avoided the logical and conceptual difficulties presented by infinite sets by avoiding them whenever possible. Their aversion, and that of others, to infinite sets was widespread enough and determined enough that there is even a name for it: *horror infiniti*. The aversion to things infinite, however, was not shared by the scholars of the late Middle Ages, who enjoyed working with infinite sets and infinite processes.

During the late Middle Ages mathematicians became interested in the idea of summing infinite series of numbers. The idea that it might be possible to sum infinitely many non-0 numbers and even obtain an ordinary (finite) number as a result can be a little surprising when first encountered. The surprise lies in the description of the act, not the "infinite sum" itself. Even in grade school we learn that numbers can be expressed as infinite sums. Consider, for example, the number 1/3 expressed as a decimal. The decimal representation of 1/3 is $0.\overline{33}$, of course, where the line above the 3s simply indicates that it continues to repeat indefinitely. Another way of writing this same number is

$$1/3 = 3/10 + 3/10^2 + 3/10^3 + \ldots$$

Whenever we write 1/3 in this way, we use an infinite set of positive numbers that, when added together, sum to the number 1/3. Mathematicians prefer to say that this "infinite sum" *converges* to 1/3.

Of course not every infinite set of positive numbers converges to an ordinary (finite) number. For example, if we add the number 1/2 to itself over and over again, we can make the sum larger than any preassigned positive number. It is tempting to say that the sum is infinite, but mathematicians have, through hard experience, learned to use the word *infinite* with great care. Instead they say that the sum $1/2 + 1/2 + 1/2 + \ldots$ *diverges*. The fact that the sum of infinitely many 1/2s diverges is more or less obvious, but there are sums that consist of infinitely many positive numbers for which it is not at all obvious that the sum either converges or diverges. These are the sums in which Oresme was interested. These kinds of sums have frequently proved useful in the study of natural phenomena.

Oresme studied one particular series that today is called the harmonic series. The harmonic series consists of all the numbers in the following sequence:

$$1/2, 1/3, 1/4, 1/5, \dots$$

There are infinitely many terms in the harmonic sequence—one term for each positive whole number—and each term in the series is smaller than the one preceding it. Oresme wanted to know whether, as these terms are added together, the sum converges or diverges. It is not possible to answer the question by just "adding them up to see what happens." The first million terms of this series, for example, add up to a number that is less than 15. Nevertheless, Oresme showed that the harmonic series diverges: That is, if we choose any number—say, for purposes of illustration, we choose the number 1,000—and we add together enough of the terms in the harmonic series, the sum exceeds 1,000. Oresme's demonstration is simply a clever way of grouping the terms in the series as he adds them.

Oresme groups the terms as follows:

$$1/2 + (1/3 + 1/4) + (1/5 + 1/6 + 1/7 + 1/8) + \dots$$

where each successive set of parentheses holds twice as many terms as the pair of parentheses preceding it. Next Oresme reasons that the sum inside each pair of parentheses is at least as large as 1/2. For example, the sum inside the first set of parentheses is slightly larger than 1/4 + 1/4, which, of course, is just another way of writing 1/2. The sum inside the second set of parentheses is at least as large as 1/8 + 1/8 + 1/8 + 1/8, because each of the four terms inside this set of parentheses is greater than or equal to 1/8. Therefore the sum inside the second set of parentheses also exceeds 1/2.

In fact the sum of the terms inside each successive set of parentheses is always at least as large as 1/2. Moreover, because there are infinitely many terms in the harmonic series, Oresme's method can be continued indefinitely. This shows that the sum of the harmonic series is at least as large as 1/2 + 1/2 + 1/2 + . . ., and as we have already noted, this sum *diverges.* In other words if we add together enough terms of the series, the sum is larger than any number that we choose. This concludes Oresme's proof.

Oresme did not try to apply his discoveries to scientific problems. He seemed more interested in the series themselves than in any possible uses that they might have. The introduction of infinite series and other "infinite processes" would, however, have a profound impact on the development of Western science and technology.

Nicolaus Copernicus

One of the most prominent of all scientific figures during this time of transition is the Polish astronomer, doctor, and lawyer Nicolaus Copernicus (1473–1543). Copernicus lived at a time when most Europeans believed that Earth is situated at the center of the universe and that the Sun, planets, and stars revolve around it. Copernicus disagreed. Today his name is synonymous with the idea that Earth and all the other planets in the solar system revolve about the Sun. He was, as we soon see, a cautious man, but his writings had revolutionary effects on the science and philosophy of Europe and, eventually, the world at large. His major work, *De Revolutionibus Orbium Coelestium* (On the revolutions of the celestial spheres), formed the basis of what is now known as the Copernican revolution.

Copernicus was born into a wealthy family. His uncle, Łukasz Watzenrode, was a bishop in the Catholic Church. Watzenrode took an interest in his nephew and helped him obtain both an excellent education and, after he finished his formal education, a secure job within the church. As a young man Copernicus traveled widely in search of the best possible education. He attended the University at Kraków, a prestigious Polish university, for four

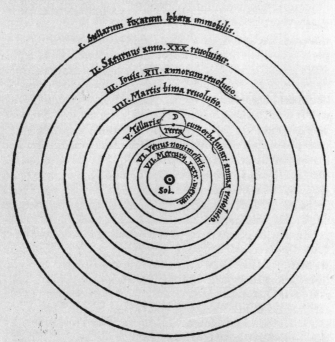

This illustration from Copernicus's De Revolutionibus Orbium Coelestium, *published in 1543, shows seven planets moving in perfectly circular orbits about the Sun.* (Library of Congress, Prints and Photographs Division)

years. He did not graduate. Instead he left for Italy, where he continued his studies. While attending the University of Bologna, he stayed at the home of a university mathematics professor, Domenico Maria de Navara, and it was there that Copernicus developed a deep interest in mathematics and astronomy. Furthermore it was with his host that he made his first astronomical observation. Together Copernicus and de Navara observed the occultation of the star Aldebaran by the Moon. (To say that Aldebaran was *occulted* by the Moon means that the Moon passed between Aldebaran and the observer, so that for a time Aldebaran was obscured by the Moon.) Copernicus's observation of Aldebaran's occultation is important not only because it was Copernicus's first observation, but also because for an astronomer he made relatively few observations over the course of his life. In fact throughout his life he published only 27 of his observations, although he made others. Although Copernicus was clearly aware of the need for more frequent and more accurate observations, he did not spend much time systematically observing the heavens himself.

In addition to his time at Bolgna Copernicus studied at the Italian universities of Padua and Ferrara. While he was in Italy he studied medicine and canon law, which is the law of the Catholic Church. At Ferrara he received a doctorate in canon law. When he returned to Poland in 1503, he was—from the point of view of early 16th-century Europe—an expert in every field of academic importance: astronomy, mathematics, medicine, and theology.

Copernicus wrote several books and published a few of them. He wrote two books about astronomy, but he showed little enthusiasm for making those particular ideas public. His first book on astronomy is *De Hypothesibus Motuum Coelestium a Se Constitutes Commentariolus* (A commentary on the theories of the motions of heavenly objects from their arrangements). It is usually called the *Commentariolus*. This short text contains Copernicus's core idea: The Sun is fixed and the planets move in circular orbits about the Sun. Copernicus attributes night and day to the revolution of Earth about its axis, and he attributes the yearly astronomical cycle to the motion of Earth about the Sun. These were important ideas, but they did not receive a wide audience because Copernicus never published this book. He was content to show the manuscript to a small circle of friends. The first time the book was published was in the 19th century, more than 300 years after it was written.

Copernicus continued to refine his ideas about astronomy and began to buttress them with mathematical arguments. His major work, *De Revolutionibus Orbium Coelestium* (On the revolutions of the celestial spheres), was completed sometime around 1530, but he did not even try to publish this work until many years later. (The book was finally published in 1543, and it is an oft-repeated story that Copernicus received his own copy on the last day of his life.)

It is in *De Revolutionibus Orbium Coelestium* that Copernicus advances his central theory, a theory that is sometimes more complex than is generally recognized. Copernicus claims that the Sun is stationary and that the planets orbit a point near the Sun. He orders the planets correctly. Mercury is closest to the Sun, followed by Venus, Earth, Mars, Jupiter, and Saturn. This sequence stands in contrast to the prevailing idea of the time, namely, that Earth is at the center of the solar system: Mercury is the planet closest to Earth, followed by Venus, the Sun, Mars, Jupiter, and Saturn. (In both the Copernican and the ancient systems the Moon orbits Earth.)

At this level of detail Copernicus's theory sounds almost modern, but it is not. In several critical ways Copernicus still clings to the geometric ideas that one finds in Ptolemy's *Almagest*. First, as Ptolemy did, Copernicus believes that all planets move at uniform speeds along circular paths. He also knew that if Earth travels at a uniform speed along a circular path centered on the Sun, then the Sun appears to move through the sky at a constant rate. Recall that even the Mesopotamians, thousands of years before the birth of Copernicus, had established that the Sun's apparent speed across the sky varies. To account for this nonuniform motion of the Sun, Copernicus places the center of Earth's orbit at a point that is near the Sun, but not at the center of the Sun.

Second, Copernicus, as Ptolemy did, believes in celestial spheres. He believes, for example, that the stars are fixed on a huge, stationary outermost celestial sphere. The difference is that

Ptolemy's outer sphere rotates; Copernicus's theory predicts a stationary outer sphere. The idea that the stars are fixed to an outer sphere is an important characteristic of Copernican astronomy. If Earth does rotate about the Sun, then changes in Earth's location should cause the relative positions of the stars to vary when viewed from Earth. (Hold your thumb up at arm's length from your nose and alternately open and close each eye. Your thumb will appear to shift position. The reason is that you are looking at it from two distinct perspectives. The same is true of our view of the stars. As Earth moves, we view the stars from different positions in space so the stars should appear to shift position just as your thumb does and for exactly the same reason.) Neither Copernicus nor anyone else could detect this effect. Copernicus reasons that the effect exists but that the universe is much larger than had previously been assumed. If the stars are sufficiently far away the effect is too small to be detected. So one logical consequence of Copernicus's model of the solar system is a huge universe.

The third difference between Copernican thought and modern ideas about astronomy is that Copernicus does not really have any convincing theoretical ideas to counter Ptolemy's arguments against a rotating Earth (see the sidebar in the section *A Rotating Earth* in chapter 2 to read an excerpt from Ptolemy's arguments against a rotating Earth.) Of course Copernicus has to try to respond to Ptolemy's ideas. Ptolemy's model of the universe dominated European ideas about astronomy during Copernicus's time, and anyone interested enough and educated enough to read Copernicus's treatise would surely have been familiar with Ptolemy's *Almagest*.

Unfortunately Copernicus's attempts to counter Ptolemy's ideas are not based on any physical insight. Whereas Ptolemy writes that objects on the surface of a huge, rapidly rotating sphere would fly off, Copernicus responds by speculating about "natural" circular motion and asserting that objects in natural circular motion do not require forces to maintain their motion. Copernicus's ideas, like Ptolemy's, are still geometric. He has only the haziest concept of what a force is. Not surprisingly Copernicus's revolutionary ideas did not convince many people when the book was first published.

Copernicus was not the first person to suggest the idea that the Sun lies at the center of the solar system and that Earth orbits the Sun. Aristarchus of Samos had considered the same idea almost two millennia earlier. Nor was Copernicus the first to propose that day and night are caused by Earth's revolving on its own axis. The ancient Hindu astronomer and mathematician Aryabhata (C.E. 476–550) also wrote that the Earth rotates on its axis. Copernicus *was* the first European of the Renaissance to propose a heliocentric, or Sun-centered, model of the universe. (A more accurate term is *heliostatic*, since Copernicus believed that the Sun does not move and that the center of the planetary orbits is a point near but not interior to the Sun.) What makes Copernicus important is that his ideas are the ones that finally displaced older competing hypotheses.

Despite the fact that he has several fundamental properties of the solar system right, Copernicus is not a scientist in the modern sense. Much of Copernicus's great work is based on philosophical and aesthetic *preferences* rather than scientific reasoning. In the absence of data there was no reason to prefer uniform circular motion to any other type of motion, but there were data. Even in Copernicus's time there were some data about the motion of the planets, and the available data *did not* support the idea of uniform circular motion. His attempts to reconcile the existing data with his aesthetic preferences for a particular geometric worldview account for much of the complexity of Copernicus's work. In spite of their weaknesses Copernicus's ideas were soon circulated widely. His book provided insight and inspiration to many scientists and philosophers, among them Galileo Galilei and Johannes Kepler. *De Revolutionibus Orbium Coelestium* was the beginning of a reevaluation of humanity's place in the universe.

Johannes Kepler

Nicolaus Copernicus took many years of effort to arrive at his heliostatic model of the solar system, whereas the young German astronomer, mathematician, and physicist Johannes Kepler (1571–1630) began his studies with Copernicus's model of the solar system. Kepler was born into a poor family. Fortunately he was also a quick study and a hard worker. He attracted the attention of the local ruling class, and they provided him with the money necessary to attend school. In 1587 Kepler enrolled at the University of Tübingen, where he studied astronomy, but Kepler had originally planned to become a minister. His first interest was theology.

By the time Kepler entered university, Copernicus had been dead 44 years. The Copernican revolution had had a slow start. Most astronomers still believed that the Sun orbits Earth. Fortunately for Kepler his astronomy professor, Michael Mästlin, was one of that minority of astronomers who believed that the main elements of Copernicus's theory were correct. Mästlin communicated these ideas to Kepler, and Kepler began to think about a problem that would occupy him for the rest of his life.

Kepler did not immediately recognize the important role astronomy would play in his life. For the next few years he continued to train for the ministry, but his mathematical talents were well known, and when the position of mathematics instructor became available at a high school in Graz, Austria, the faculty at Tübingen recommended him for the post. He left without completing his advanced studies in theology. He never did become a minister.

Kepler's first attempt at understanding the geometry of the solar system was, in a philosophical way, reminiscent of that of the ancient Greeks. To understand his idea we need to remember that the only planets known at the time were Mercury, Venus, Earth, Mars, Jupiter, and Saturn. We also need to know that he was at this time a true Copernican in the sense that he, as Copernicus did, believed that the planets are attached to rotating spheres. Finally, we also need to know something about Platonic solids.

We are all familiar with regular polygons. There are infinitely many, differently shaped, regular polygons. Every regular polygon is a plane figure characterized by the fact that all its sides are of equal length and all the interior angles are of equal measure. Equilateral triangles, squares, and (regular) pentagons and hexagons are all examples of common regular polygons. More generally in two dimensions there is a regular polygon with any number of sides. In three dimensions the situation is different. In three dimensions the analog of a regular polygon is a three-dimensional solid called a Platonic solid. A Platonic solid is a three-dimensional figure with flat faces and straight edges. Each face of a Platonic solid is the same size and shape as every other face. Each edge is the same length as every other edge, and the angles at which the faces of a particular Platonic solid are joined are also identical. Platonic solids are as regular in three dimensions as regular polygons are "regular"

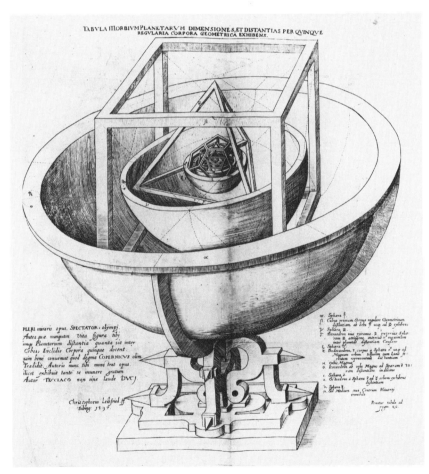

A diagram of Johannes Kepler's early concept of the solar system, in which he used Platonic solids to describe the relative distances of the six known planets from the Sun (Hulton Archive/Getty Images)

in two. There are only five Platonic solids: the tetrahedron, cube, octahedron, dodecahedron, and icosahedron. Kepler believed that the Platonic solids could be used to describe the shape of the solar system.

As far as Kepler knew, there are only six planets. He knew a little about the ratios of the distances between the planetary spheres, and he had an idea that the distances between the spheres, to which he believed the planets are attached, might somehow be related to the five Platonic solids. His goal, then, was to explain the distances between the planets in terms of the Platonic solids. He did this by nesting the Platonic solids inside the planetary spheres. Because the Platonic solids are regular, there is exactly one largest sphere that can fit inside each solid (provided, of course, that we imagine each solid as having a hollow interior) and one smallest sphere that can contain that solid. For example the smallest sphere that can contain a cube touches each of the eight corners of the cube. This arrangement is described by saying that the cube is circumscribed by the sphere. The largest sphere that can fit inside the cube—called the inscribed sphere—touches the center of each of the interior walls of the cube. What Kepler discovered is that if he alternately nested spheres and Platonic solids, one inside the other—and he nested them in the right order—then the ratios of the distances of the spheres from the center of his model were a "pretty good" fit for the ratios of the distances of the planets from the Sun! It is an extraordinary fact that Kepler's scheme does, indeed, yield a reasonably good fit. Given the uncertainties about planetary distances that existed at the time, it must have appeared to him that he had discovered a fundamental law of nature.

Kepler's discovery is fortuitous. His "reasoning" about Platonic solids is pure Pythagorean mysticism. Though Kepler is best remembered for his later discoveries about the true nature of planetary motion, he was always very fond of these mystical geometric descriptions and incorporated them in all of his major works. Throughout his life Kepler firmly straddled the boundary between the world of the ancients and the fast-evolving world of what we now call modern science.

Kepler's ideas about the role of Platonic solids in the geometry of the solar system attracted the attention of the Danish astronomer Tycho Brahe (1546–1601). Brahe had an observatory—perhaps the best observatory in the world at the time—and assistants. He and his staff made an extraordinary number of measurements of the positions of all known planets plus hundreds of stars. They were creative in designing and building new instruments to aid them in their measurements. Brahe amassed a large number of highly accurate naked-eye measurements.

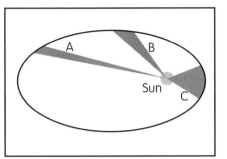

Kepler's later model of the solar system conserved areas. The Sun is at the apex of each "slice," and the ellipse marks the orbital path of the planet:
a. Areas A, B, and C are equal.
b. The times the planet takes to move along arcs A, B, and C are the same.
c. Therefore the planet moves faster when it is closer to the Sun than when it is farther away.

(The telescope had not yet been invented.) Kepler soon found a position on Brahe's staff, and later when Brahe died, Kepler took Brahe's measurements with him. He spent years analyzing the data therein while trying to develop a model of planetary motion that would account for these observations. The resulting model of planetary motion, called Kepler's three laws of planetary motion, asserts that

1. Each planet moves in an elliptical orbit with the Sun at one focus.

2. The line that joins a planet to the Sun sweeps out equal areas in equal times.

3. The square of the length of each planet's year, T^2, when T is measured in Earth years, equals the cube of the average distance of that planet to the Sun, D^3, where D is measured in multiples of Earth's distance from the Sun. In symbols, $D^3 = T^2$.

D, DISTANCE FROM SUN		**T,** ORBITAL PERIOD	**D³/T²**
(In multiples of Earth - Sun distance)		(In multiples of Earth years)	(Distance cubed / time squared)
Mercury	0.386	0.241	0.990
Venus	0.72	0.615	0.987
Earth	1	1	1
Mars	1.52	1.88	0.994
Jupiter	5.2	11.86	1
Saturn	9.54	29.46	1
Uranus	19.18	84.01	1
Neptune	30.06	164.79	1
Pluto	39.43	248	0.997

Kepler's laws are qualitatively different from previous astronomical discoveries. Ptolemy and Copernicus, for example, both searched for explanations for previously observed planetary phenomena. Neither of their theories was predictive in the sense that they could accommodate new discoveries. Had Ptolemy discovered a new planet he would have had to begin again—imagining one sphere revolving about another and another until he found the right combination to describe the motion of the new planet with acceptable accuracy. Similarly Copernicus's theory had no real predictive capability. But Kepler's laws do generalize: They were used successfully more than 150 years after Kepler's death to learn about the average distance from the Sun to the newly discovered planet Uranus. Scientists measured Uranus's orbital period and then computed its distance with the help of Kepler's third law. So Kepler's laws applied to a planet that Kepler never even knew existed! It should be noted, however, that Kepler's laws contain no concept of mass, energy, or momentum. He theory is still a purely geometric one.

To appreciate Kepler's first law, knowing some of the geometry of ellipses and the relationship of an ellipse to a circle is helpful. Recall that an ellipse is formed by choosing a length and two points. The points are called the foci of the ellipse. A third point, *P,* is on the ellipse if the sum of the distances from *P* to the foci equals the given length. The ellipse is exactly the set of points that

PLATONIC SOLIDS

The Greeks discovered all five of the Platonic solids: the tetrahedron, cube, octahedron, dodecahedron, and icosahedron. Each face of a Platonic solid is a regular polygon of some type, and each face is identical to every other face (see the diagram). Moreover, for any particular Platonic solid, the angle at which two faces meet is the same for any pair of sides. It has long been known that there are exactly five such solids that meet these restrictions. The Greeks attached a lot of significance to these five geometrical forms. They believed that the Platonic solids represent the basic elements of which the world is made. The Greek philosopher Plato (ca. 427 B.C.E.–ca. 347 B.C.E.) believed that the cube represented Earth, the icosahedron represented water, the tetrahedron fire, and the octahedron air. For Plato geometric shapes were firmly intertwined with his concept of chemistry. Plato's ideas persisted right into the European Enlightenment of the 17th and 18th centuries. (In fact even Isaac Newton, the great 17th-century British physicist and

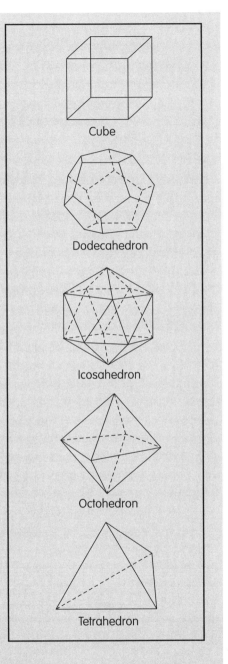

Cube

Dodecahedron

Icosahedron

Octohedron

Tetrahedron

The five Platonic solids (above right)   **(continues)**

PLATONIC SOLIDS
(continued)

mathematician, took the existence of the four "elements" quite seriously.) Plato was less sure of the role of the dodecahedron, but later Greek philosophers took it to represent the "aether," the material that supposedly fills the heavens. (The idea of aether was not abandoned until the early years of the 20th century.) These mystical speculations about the properties of geometric forms and their relationship to the physical world have persisted in one form or another for most of the last few thousand years.

meet this criterion. The distance between the foci also helps to determine the shape of the ellipse: If the length does not change, then the closer the foci are to one another, the more closely the ellipse approximates a circle. If the foci are pushed together until they coincide, the ellipse *is* a circle. This means that a circle is a very specific type of ellipse. In this sense Kepler's model is a generalization of the Copernican model.

Kepler did not readily embrace the idea of elliptical planetary orbits. In fact it was years before Kepler abandoned the idea of circular orbits, but there was no way that he could reconcile circular planetary orbits with the data that he inherited from Brahe. He eventually concluded that the data were best explained by the hypothesis that planets move along elliptical paths and that the center of the Sun always occupies one focus of each ellipse. This is Kepler's first law.

The second law describes how the planets follow their elliptical paths. Earlier in his life when Kepler still subscribed to the idea that planets moved along circular paths at constant velocities, he believed that they moved equal distances along their orbits in equal times. Another way of expressing this old-fashioned idea is that a line connecting a planet with the Sun sweeps out, or covers, equal areas of the enclosed circle in equal times—one-quarter of the inside of the circle, for example, is swept out in one-quarter of that planet's year. For a planet moving at constant speed along a circular path, one statement—the planet moves at constant speed—implies the other—equal areas are swept out in equal times. The situation is only a little more complicated for elliptical orbits. Brahe's data showed that the speed of each planet changes as it moves along its elliptical path, so it cannot be true that a planet moves equal distances in equal times. What Kepler discovered, however, is that the speed of each planet changes in such a way that it still sweeps out equal areas in equal times. Distances are not conserved, but (swept out) areas continue to be conserved under Kepler's model. Again Kepler's model is a generalization of Copernicus's model.

Finally, Kepler's third law is a statement about the relationship between each planet-to-Sun distance and the length of that planet's year. The ratio Kepler discovered is most easily expressed if we measure each planet's year as a multiple of an Earth year and if we measure each planet-to-Sun distance as a multiple of the Earth-to-Sun distance. Kepler asserts that the square of the length of a planet's year equals the cube of its distance from the Sun, where we measure both quantities as described in the preceding sentence. The third law is very useful, because it says that if we know how long a planet takes to orbit the Sun, then *we can compute* the distance of that planet to the Sun. It is relatively easy to compute the length of a planet's year. We simply measure how fast it changes its position relative to the background stars. This enables us to determine how many degrees it is moving per Earth-day, and from this we can compute how many Earth-days are required for it to move 360°. These techniques enabled astronomers to determine relative distances of planets in the solar system (see the accompanying chart).

Kepler's laws are not exact, as the accompanying chart indicates; nor is there any additional information in his theory that would allow us to improve upon these results. The discrepancies result from small irregularities in each planet's orbit. These irregularities cannot be predicted from Kepler's theory of planetary motion. They are the result of gravitational interactions between the planets. Nevertheless, the chart shows that despite all that Kepler did not know, his description of planetary motion is remarkably accurate.

Leonardo da Vinci and the Equation of Continuity

The Italian artist, scientist, and inventor Leonardo da Vinci (1452–1519) is one of the great icons of Western culture. All sorts of accomplishments are regularly attributed to him. He has been described as a great painter, sculptor, inventor, architect, musician, meteorologist, athlete, physicist, anatomist, and engineer, and a master of many other fields as well. Never mind that we have fewer than two dozen paintings that can be attributed to him or that there is some disagreement among scholars about whether some of those paintings are his work at all. He left detailed drawings of an enormous monument, but no monument. He left numerous illustrations of buildings and inventions but little in the way of actual architecture and few actual devices. What we do have are his notebooks. The notebooks are long, carefully illustrated journals.

Leonardo began to record his ideas in journal form as a young man. It was a practice that he followed for the rest of his life. The notebooks detail his ideas about a wide variety of fields. It is in the notebooks that we find what could have been his contributions to the development of art, engineering, science, and many other fields. The notebooks were preserved but not published until long after his death. His ideas were not widely circulated during his lifetime, and they had little effect on his contemporaries or on the subsequent history of science. Nevertheless, in one of his notebooks we find what is perhaps the first instance of a conservation law, and because so much of the physical sciences is expressed in terms of conservation laws, it is well worth our time to study Leonardo's thinking on this matter.

Leonardo was born in Anchiano near the city of Vinci. We do not know much about Leonardo's early life. He apparently demonstrated his artistic talent at a young age, and sometime around the age of 15 he was apprenticed to a prominent Florentine artist named Andrea Verrocchio (1435–88). (Apprenticeship was the usual way that the artists of Leonardo's time and place were educated.) Verrocchio had a large studio and he received many important commissions for paintings and sculptures. In addition to Leonardo, Verrocchio taught Perugino, who would later become master to the great painter Raphael. Verrocchio also worked closely with Sandro Botticelli, one of the major painters of the time, and Domenico Ghirlandajo, who would later become master to Michelangelo.

Leonardo apparently enjoyed the busy and creative environment of Verrocchio's studio. In 1472 Leonardo was admitted to the Guild of Saint Luke as a painter. Although it was common for artists to open their own studios once they were admitted to a guild, Leonardo remained at Verrocchio's studio for five additional years before striking out on his own.

As an independent artist Leonardo won many important commissions, only some of which he completed. He moved several times—he eventually died in France—and he became well known as both an artist and a highly original inventor and scientist. Leonardo's adult life was marked by the intense study of many different branches of knowledge. Unlike many of his predecessors, Leonardo looked for underlying principles. He searched for certainty, and he believed that no knowledge that was not founded on mathematics could be certain.

Leonardo was fascinated with fluids—gases as well as liquids—and he recognized the importance of mathematics as a language in which to express his ideas about fluids. Leonardo was not an especially adept mathematician, but his emphasis on mathematics was for the time very forward-thinking. He clearly had a mathematical bent. He enjoyed thinking about problems that today we generally express mathematically. He wrote about how to control the flow of rivers. He designed numerous flying machines. He studied the motion of waves. Leonardo's writings were not idle speculation, nor were they simply fantasy. He had real insight into the field that we now call fluid dynamics. Even so, many of the problems of most interest to him were just too hard for him to solve. The mathematics of the day was simply not advanced enough to express the ideas that he had in mind; nor did Leonardo contribute much in the way of new mathematics himself.

Leonardo's contribution to science that is of most interest to us is sometimes called the velocity-area law. Sometimes his discovery is called the equation of continuity, although there are other, much more general versions of the equation of continuity in use today. Whatever we call it, Leonardo's insight is a nice example of the transition from geometrical to physical thinking that was going on in Renaissance Europe at this time.

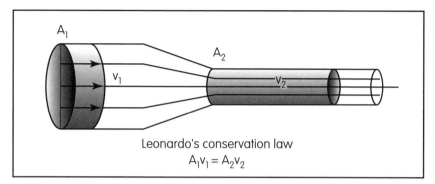

Diagram illustrating Leonardo's conservation of volume law. We write as an equation: $A_1v_1 = A_2v_2$.

The velocity-area law states that the velocity of water at any location along a channel where water is flowing at a steady rate is inversely proportional to the cross-sectional area of the channel. In symbols it is often expressed as $Av = V$, where A is the cross-sectional area of the channel at the location of interest, v is the velocity of the water at that same location, and V is called the volumetric flow rate. The symbol V represents the volume of water flowing past any point on the channel per unit of time. Leonardo has reduced the problem of water flowing down a channel to an algebraic equation. There are three variables in one equation, so if we can measure any two of the variables, we can compute the third. For example, if we can find V at any point along the channel, and we can measure the cross-sectional area, A, of the channel at some point of interest, then we can compute the velocity of the water at that point by dividing both sides by A: $v = V/A$. This is physics reduced to mathematics, and in that respect it is very modern.

To appreciate Leonardo's idea better, we need to understand his two basic assumptions. Leonardo's first assumption is that the flow of the water along the channel is time-independent, or, to express the idea in different but equivalent language: The flow is *steady-state*. This means that the volume of water flowing past a particular location in the channel does not change with time. In particular there are no places along the channel where water is "backing up."

In Leonardo's model it is always true that at every instant of time the volumetric flow into one section of the channel equals the volumetric flow out of any other section.

Second, Leonardo assumes that water is incompressible. This means that no matter how we squeeze or push on a particular mass of water, its volume—if not its shape—remains unchanged. Leonardo's model is, of course, an idealization. It is not strictly true that water is incompressible. It is always possible to expand or compress a volume of water, but in many practical situations the resulting change in volume of a mass of water is small. For the types of applications that Leonardo had in mind, only small inaccuracies are introduced by imagining that water is incompressible. The advantage of deliberately incorporating this inaccuracy into his mathematical model is that if one assumes that water is incompressible, the resulting equation is much easier to solve, and the solutions are still reasonably accurate.

The big difference between Leonardo's ideas and a modern formulation of the same problem is that Leonardo emphasizes the geometric property of volume as opposed to the physical property of mass. Scientists and engineers today consider mass more fundamental than volume. Consequently they usually express Leonardo's relationship in terms of the rate of mass flow rather than volume flow. Remember, however, that one of Leonardo's assumptions is that water is incompressible. Under these conditions the mass is proportional to the volume, so what is true of the volume is equally true of the mass. For Leonardo the two formulations are equivalent. This is part of the beauty and utility of Leonardo's discovery.

Leonardo was the first to formulate a simple conservation equation and to exploit the equation to understand the flow better. What is important for our story is that Leonardo located a property, volumetric flow, that is invariant from one point along the channel to another. In his model volume is conserved provided his assumptions about the nature of the flow are satisfied. The search for conserved properties would soon occupy many of the best scientific minds. The concept of conserved quantities continues to occupy the attention of scientists and engineers in our own time.

PROVING LEONARDO'S EQUATION OF CONTINUITY

It may not be obvious how the final equation $Av = V$ came about; it may even seem to be a lucky guess. But Leonardo's equation of continuity can be proved with only a little effort. Suppose that we measure a volume of fluid moving down a channel. We can call this amount of fluid M. For example, if we turn on a hose, M would represent the volume of water that had flowed out of the hose during the time interval of interest. We can represent the amount of time required for M to pass a particular point on the channel by the letter t. To return to the hose example, if M represented a bucketful of water, t would represent the amount of time required to fill the bucket. The volumetric rate of flow, V, is *defined* as M/t. The volume of water as it flows along the channel (or hose) has a certain shape. The volume, M, of the water in the channel equals the cross-sectional area of the channel multiplied by the length of the cylinder of fluid whose volume is M

$$M = AL$$

where A is the cross-sectional area of the channel and L is the length of the cylinder. If we divide both sides of this equation by t we get

$$M/t = AL/t$$

Finally, we need to notice that M/t *is* V, the volumetric rate of flow, and L/t is the velocity at which the water flows past the point of interest. Our conclusion is that

$$V = Av$$

We make use of Leonardo's equation of continuity whenever we force water to shoot forcefully out of the end of a hose by constricting the hose's opening.

Conceptually the work of the scientists in this chapter forms a bridge between the older, geometric ideas of the Greeks and the more modern, physical ideas of scientists such as Galileo and Simon Stevin, who were soon to follow. The scientists described were willing to look at nature in new ways, but they did not recognize the importance of force, mass, and energy. As did the Greeks, they still thought of geometry as the central organizing principle of nature. Their ideas would soon be pushed aside some-what by the new science, which relied on "conservation laws" to explore nature. Interestingly geometry would again come to the fore in the early 20th century when Emmy Noether established that conservation laws imply certain geometric symmetries, and vice versa. For the time being, however, the work of these scientists represented the end of an era that stretched back to ancient Greece.

4

NEW SCIENCES

One characteristic that all of the scientists and mathematicians whose work has been examined so far have in common is that they were primarily interested in developing geometric descriptions of nature. Leonardo's conservation law is a conservation of volume law. Johannes Kepler's third law of planetary motion is essentially a conservation of area law. Both Kepler and Leonardo speculated about the concept of force, but neither developed a useful concept of force. Even Archimedes, whose buoyancy law successfully describes the nature of the buoyancy force, may have been successful because he was able to relate the buoyancy force to the volume occupied by the submerged object. In any case Archimedes did not continue beyond his treatment of the buoyancy force to develop a more general concept of force. (In his treatment of the lever force is a consequence of the symmetry of the geometric configuration of the lever.)

Conditions began to change rapidly even during Kepler's lifetime with the work of the Flemish mathematician, scientist, engineer, and inventor Simon Stevin (1548–1620) and the Italian mathematician, scientist, and inventor Galileo Galilei (1564–1642). The ideas and discoveries of these two individuals profoundly influenced many aspects of life in Europe, and today their influence can be felt around the world. It was not just their discoveries that mattered. It was also their approach. Over the succeeding centuries Galileo and Stevin's concept of what science is has proved at least as important as their discoveries. Both Galileo and Stevin combined rigorous mathematics with carefully designed and executed experiments to reveal new aspects of nature and,

DE LA SPARTOSTATIQUE.

COROLLAIRE III.

Or pour venir à la declaration de la qualité des pe-
santeurs suspenduës par cordages, soit AB une colomne,
de laquelle C soit le centre, suspenduë à deux lignes
CD, CE (venans dudit centre C) és poincts ferm es
D, E, lesquels seront diametres de gravité par la 5 definition: parquoy menant HI
entre DC, CF, parallele à
CE, alors par la 13 definition, CI sera elevation droite, CH oblique; tellement
que comme CI à CH, ainsi
cest elevant direct à l'elevant
oblique: mais l'elevant direct
de CI est egal au poids de la
colomne: Donc comme CI
à CH, ainsi le poids de la
colomne entiere, au poids
qui avient en D; & de mes-
me maniere trouvera-on le poids qui advient en E, en
menant de I jusques à CE, la ligue IK, parallele à DC;
& disant, comme l'elevation droite CI à l'elevation
oblique CK, ainsi le poids de la colomne, au poids qui
advient sur E.

Mais CK est tousjours egale à HI; parquoy il n'est
pas besoing de mener ceste ligne derniere IK, car sans
cela les termes necessaires sont cognus au triangle HIC,
avec lequel on dira: comme CI à CH, ainsi le poids
de la colomne, au poids qui advient sur D. D'avantage
CI à IH, ainsi le poids de la colomne, au poids qui
advient sur E. Derechef comme CH à HI, ainsi le poids
qui advient sur D, au poids qui advient sur E.

COROLLAIRE IV.

Et pour proceder plus avant, soit AB la colomne
abaissée, comme cy joignant, & par la troisiesme peti-

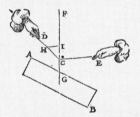

tion, il n'y a en cela aucune alteration, & partant la
mesme proportion que dessus y sera encore.

COROLLAIRE V.

Soit maintenant au lieu de la colomne precedente,
un corps d'egale pesanteur à icelle, de figure & matiere

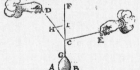

quelconque, alors la mesme proportion demeurera;
assavoir, comme CI à IH, ainsi AB au poids qui ad-

vient en E. Derechef comme CH à HI, ainsi le poids
que D soustient, à celuy que E soustient.

D'icy est manifeste, que s'il y avoit à la ligne DCE
comme corde, un poids AB cognu, & les angles FCD,
FCE, aussi cognus, qu'on pourra dire quel poids advient sur chaque partie, comme DC, CE.

COROLLAIRE VI.

Mais s'il y avoit plusieurs poids suspendus en une
mesme ligne, comme icy la ligne ABCDEF, ses poincts
fermes extremes A, F, à laquelle sont suspendus 4 poids
cognus, G, H, I, K; il est manifeste qu'on peut dire
quel effort ils font à la corde, à chacune de ses parties
AB, BC, CD, DE, EF: Car par exemple, produisant
GB enhaut vers L, & MN parallele à BC: Je dis BN
donne BM, combien le poids G? viendra l'effort qui
est fait à AB.

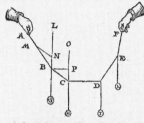

Derechef BN donne MN, combien le poids G?
ce qui viendra sera l'effort qui est fait à BC.

Soit encore HC produite jusques en O, & BP parallele à GD: Je dis alors, CP donne CB, combien le
poids H? Ce qui en sortira sera pour la force qui eschoir
sur BC, d'où s'ensuit, qu'il faudra trouver le mesme
qu'à BC cy-dessus. De ces choses, & de plusieurs autres
S. Excel. a trouvé que la practique s'accorde du tout
avec la Theorie.

La proportion de la 27 proposition peut encor estre
autrement exposée, que cy-dessus, d'où s'ensuit une
operation plus facile. Soit par exemple la figure de la
27 proposition, où est dit, que comme l'elevant oblique
au direct, ainsi chaque elevant oblique à son elevant direct. Mais pour dire cecy d'une autre maniere, d'où

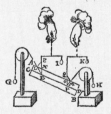

resulte une operation plus facile: Soit menée entre les
elevations droite, & oblique une ligne, comme LP,
parallele à FM: Ce qu'estant ainsi, je dis maintenant,
que comme l'elevation directe, à l'elevation oblique,
ainsi la pesanteur de la colomne entiere, à son elevant
oblique;

A page from Stevin's De la Spartostatique, *published in 1634, demonstrating his understanding of forces* (Library of Congress, Prints and
Photographs division)

sometimes, new aspects of mathematics as well. This careful combination of experimental science and rigorous mathematical modeling characterizes today's physical sciences as well as many aspects of the life sciences.

It was a central tenet of the work of Galileo and Stevin that experimental demonstrations should be *reproducible*. If one doubted their conclusions one could always check the experiments for oneself. Reproducibility served to diminish the importance of authority. No matter how important, powerful, or revered someone might be; no matter how highly regarded the scientific ideas of an individual might be, all scientific ideas were open to scrutiny and experimental testing by *anyone* with sufficient knowledge, equipment, and technique to devise and perform the necessary experiments. Just as important: If experimental results conflicted with theory, it was the theory, rather than the experimental evidence, that had to be modified or rejected. This principle applied to all scientific theories proposed by anyone. Galileo and Stevin were two of the great revolutionaries of their time. Galileo, who lived in an authoritarian society, faced severe persecution for his revolutionary views. Stevin, who lived in a far more tolerant society, was richly rewarded for his.

Simon Stevin

Simon Stevin, also known as Stevinus, was born in Bruges, Belgium, a city to which he felt very close all of his life and where he is still fondly remembered today. Stevin was a member of a poor family and began his adult life as a bookkeeper. He also worked as a clerk. Both jobs required him to be handy with figures, and his experiences must have influenced his later ideas on the importance of the decimalization of the number system. Stevin eventually left Bruges to settle in Leiden in what is now the Netherlands. At the age of 35 he enrolled as a student at the University of Leiden, where he began a lifelong friendship with Prince Maurice of Nassau. He eventually became tutor, engineer, and adviser to the prince.

Maurice of Nassau was an important military leader in the war of independence that Holland fought against Spain, called the Eighty Years' War. Much of the warfare of this time consisted of siege warfare, and Stevin had a particular genius for designing fortifications and for using water as a weapon. Stevin developed the tactic of flooding selected areas of Holland to drive off the Spanish. As a military engineer

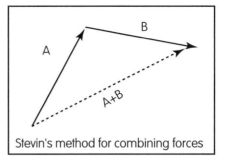

Stevin's method for combining forces

Stevin invented an arithmetic law of forces that enabled him to compute the effect of two forces acting at a point.

Stevin played an important role in many Dutch victories, and he was richly rewarded for his services, but Stevin was more than simply a military engineer. As many good Dutch engineers have been throughout the history of the Netherlands, he was interested in the construction of dykes and sluices and in the harnessing of wind to do work. He was a creative inventor and designer in this regard. He is generally credited with discovering the law of the inclined plane. All of this was important, of course, but in his own time Stevin was best known to the general public as the designer of a large, sail-powered wagon that carried Maurice of Nassau and several friends up and down the beach at the unheard-of speed of 20 mph (32 kph).

Today Stevin is best remembered for his discoveries in mathematics and in the science of statics, that branch of physics that deals with the forces that exist in bodies that are in a state of rest. For Stevin making progress in science often required making simultaneous progress in mathematics. In his study of statics Stevin formulated a rigorous description of how forces combine. Unlike Leonardo, who thought long and hard about what forces *are*, Stevin was concerned with how forces interact. This emphasis is much closer to a modern viewpoint. In the same way that the concepts of point, line, and plane are fundamental to Euclidean geometry, forces are fundamental to Stevin's concept of physics.

Stevin's best-known discovery is usually described as the parallelogram of forces. Although Stevin actually used a triangle rather than a parallelogram to express his idea, the two formulations of his discovery are completely equivalent. To motivate his idea Stevin imagined a long chain with the property that the two ends are joined to form one large loop. Now suppose that a chain is hanging motionless from a triangular support oriented so that the bottom side of the triangle is parallel to the ground. At this point the forces acting on the chain are in equilibrium. The proof of this statement *is* that the chain hangs motionless off the support. If it were not in equilibrium, it would be in motion.

If now the chain is simultaneously cut at the two lower vertices of the triangle, the bottom part of the chain falls away and the upper part remains motionless. The top part of the chain remains in equilibrium. The pulling force exerted by the segment of chain on the right leg of the triangle against the section of chain on the left leg of the triangle exactly balances the pulling force exerted by the segment of chain on the left. As Stevin knew, there is nothing special about a chain. For him it was just a conceptual aid. If we replace the chain segments by any two other objects connected by a string—and we choose the new objects so that the ratio of their weights equals the ratio of the weights of the chain segments resting on the legs of the triangle—the system remains in equilibrium. Stevin's model reveals how forces with different strengths and directions—here represented by the weights of chain segments lying on differently inclined surfaces—combine.

Stevin's force diagram gave rise to the idea of representing forces by arrows or *vectors*. The direction of each arrow or vector indicates the direction of the force. The strength of the force is proportional to the length of the arrow. Implicit in this description is the idea that a force is completely characterized by its direction and its strength. In this approach combining two forces is a simple matter of placing them "head to tail." The sum of the two vectors is the single force vector with tail at the tail of the initial vector and head at the head of the final vector in the diagram. The value of Stevin's discovery is that it gives rise to a simple and accurate method of representing, and arithmetically manipulating, forces. Stevin invented an arithmetic in which the objects acted upon are not numbers but vectors. His graphical representation of forces also allowed a relatively simple geometric interpretation of a complex system of forces. His innovation greatly facilitated the study of statics.

Stevin's second contribution to the study of statics was in the area of hydrostatics, the study of fluids at rest. Part of the value of Stevin's discoveries in the field of hydrostatics arises out of insights he gained into the physics of fluids, but there is more to this work than science. Part of the value of his work lies in the mathematical methods he invented to learn about fluids. We give one especially important example of the type of result that he achieved in this area.

Imagine a body of water at rest and held in place by a vertical wall. The wall can be a dam, a dyke, or one side of a rectangular container. Stevin wanted to know how much force the water exerted on the wall. The difficulty arises from the fact that the pressure the water exerts against the wall is not constant along the wall. The pressure, which is the force per unit area that is exerted by the water at each point along the wall, depends on how far below the surface that point is located. The farther below the surface the point is located, the greater the pressure the water exerts at that position. If we double the depth, we double the pressure. Stevin knew all of this before he began. What he did not know was the *total* force exerted by the water on the wall. This was the quantity he wanted to compute.

To understand Stevin's insight suppose that we already know (or have measured) the pressure that the water exerts at the bottom of our wall. We call that pressure P, the maximal pressure exerted by the water against the wall. If we multiply the area of the wall, which we call A, by the pressure *at the base of the wall*, we get an overestimate of the force exerted by the water. We can write our overestimate as $P \times A$. If we multiply the area of the wall by the pressure exerted by the water *at the surface of the water*—at the surface the water exerts 0 pressure—then our estimate of the total force exerted by the water on the wall is 0. This is clearly an underestimate. Neither estimate is very accurate, of course, but the idea of making simple over- and underestimates is almost enough to solve the problem.

STEVIN AND MUSIC

An interesting and less well-known contribution of Simon Stevin to Western culture is related to music as well as mathematics. More than 2,000 years before Stevin's birth a group of Greek philosopher-mathematicians under the leadership of Pythagoras of Samos discovered a simple relationship between conso-nant or harmonious sounds and the ratios of the lengths of a string. The device they used to explore these ratios is called a monochord, which is a little like a one-string steel guitar. Between the two ends of the string they placed a movable bridge. The bridge divided the string into two independently vibrating segments. They would then simultaneously

Stevin advocated the adoption of the system of musical tuning that today characterizes virtually all of Western music. (Library of Congress, Prints and Photographs Division)

pluck the string on both sides of the bridge and listen to the resulting har-monies. The Pythagoreans discovered that if the string is stopped exact-ly in the middle so that the lengths of the string on each side of the bridge are in the ratio 1:1, then the sound produced when both parts of the string are plucked is harmonious. This is called the unison. They further discovered that if the string is stopped so that the lengths of the two sides are in the ratio 1:2, a new harmonious sound is produced. We call this interval an octave. If the string is divided into lengths with the ratio 2:3 the result is what we call a perfect fifth. Finally, they discovered that

In symbols, our results, so far, look like this: $PA \geq F \geq 0$, where we let the letter F represent the total force. Notice that we have "trapped" F in the interval between 0 and PA. In mathematics, if the string is divided into lengths that are in the ratio 3:4, the result is what we call a perfect fourth. These connections between ratios and harmonies greatly influenced musicians for centuries.

The "perfect" fourths and fifths of the Pythagoreans, however, are not exactly the perfect fourths and fifths that we hear in Western music today. If we construct a scale using the Pythagorean intervals, we get a scale that is similar but not identical to the one we hear when we play a piano. Some of the frequency intervals in a scale obtained from the tuning system of the Pythagoreans are larger—and some are smaller—than the scales to which we have become accustomed. The frequency differences are, however, small enough so that on a simple melody most of us would probably not even be aware that they exist. The situation changes dramatically, however, as the harmonic and melodic components of the music become more complex. The more harmonically complex the music is, the more jarring the differences between the Pythagorean tuning and our own contemporary system of tuning become.

In Stevin's time composers were moving beyond simple melodies. They were exploring increasingly complex melodies and harmonies. They were designing musical instruments such as the harpsichord, a precursor to the piano, that require more sophisticated tuning. The traditional scales that were consequences of the natural overtone system—the Pythagorean-inspired tunings—often sounded unpleasant and distinctly out of tune on these instruments. Stevin proposed abandoning the natural overtone system of the Pythagoreans. He wanted to divide each octave into 12 equal (chromatic) steps. These are the 12 notes that the chromatic scale of Western music comprises. This change in musical intonation made it possible for composers to modulate from one key to the next in their compositions without sounding out of tune during the performance. The new system of tuning made Western music, as we know it today, possible. Stevin was a very influential proponent of equitempered tuning. Another proponent of equitempered tuning was Vincenzo Galilei, a prominent musician and composer in his own time. Today Vincenzo is remembered principally as the father of Galileo Galilei.

however, what can be done once can usually be done twice, and that is our next goal. Now imagine that we draw a line along the wall exactly halfway between the surface of the water and the base of the wall. We now repeat the procedure we just performed on each half of the wall. The results are an upper and a lower estimate for each half. If we add the halves together we get an upper and lower estimate for F, the total force exerted on the wall by the water. The procedure takes more work, but our new upper and lower estimates are closer together than the previous ones. In symbols this is the result of our second, more accurate estimate: $0.75\ PA \geq F \geq 0.25\ PA$. Notice that this time we have trapped F, the total force, in an interval that is half the size of that obtained in our first calculation. As a consequence we now know more about F than we did before.

We can continue to improve our results by dividing the wall into thinner and thinner sections. If we divide the wall, as Stevin did, into 1,000 equal horizontal strips, and compute an upper and a lower estimate for each strip, and then add them together, the result is $0.5005\ PA \geq F \geq 0.4995\ PA$. Notice how close the upper and lower estimates are now. The more finely he divides the wall, the closer the upper estimate is to the lower estimate, or to put it another way: The more finely he divides the wall, the smaller the interval containing F becomes. The only number that belongs to all such intervals is $0.5\ PA$. Stevin recognized this and concluded that the force exerted by the water on the wall is $0.5\ PA$. He was correct, but notice that no matter how finely the wall is divided, neither the lower estimate nor the upper estimate equals $0.5\ PA$. Instead Stevin's method simply "squeezes" any other possible answer out of consideration. This is a beautiful example of an algorithm that utilizes infinite processes to solve a problem in physics.

If Stevin's technique seems familiar, that may be because his method is essentially the same one employed by Archimedes to find upper and lower estimates for the number π. This technique is an early form of calculus called infinitesimal analysis. Stevin, as Archimedes was, was a master at infinitesimal analysis. What distinguishes Stevin's work from that of Archimedes is that Archimedes restricted himself to geometric methods. In this calculation Stevin used arithmetic methods in his calculations. In fact Stevin was the first mathematician to make the switch from a geometric to an arithmetic approach to infinitesimal analysis. This was an important innovation because the switch from geometry to arithmetic made these computations considerably easier.

In addition to making his mathematical innovations Stevin conducted a number of important experiments. One of his experiments links three important figures in the history of mathematics, Stevin, Galileo, and Oresme, with the Greek philosopher Aristotle. During Stevin's time it was a commonly held opinion that heavier bodies fall faster than lighter ones. This belief stemmed from the writings of Aristotle two millennia earlier. Aristotle believed that if one body is twice as heavy as a second body, then the heavier body falls at twice the speed of the lighter one. Over the intervening centuries this opinion, as many of Aristotle's opinions had, became an article of faith among well-educated Europeans. In this case, however, Aristotle had gotten it wrong. Stevin investigated the situation by simultaneously releasing two weights, one 10 times heavier than the other, and noting that they landed simultaneously (or nearly so) each time the experiment was repeated.

Most people are familiar with the story of Galileo's dropping two different sized cannonballs off the Leaning Tower of Pisa and noticing that they struck the ground simultaneously, but there is little evidence that Galileo ever performed this experiment. Cannonballs and the Leaning Tower make for great theater, of course, but even if Galileo had proven Aristotle wrong in this dramatic experiment, he would have been too late to claim priority. Stevin's experiment was performed almost two decades before Galileo began a systematic study of the physics governing falling bodies. Galileo, however, discovered *how* objects in free fall move: They accelerate at a constant rate. This discovery was the result of Galileo's own painstaking experiments. The *mathematical* description of how objects move under constant acceleration was, however, pioneered by Oresme two centuries before Stevin began his experiments.

Galileo Galilei

The Italian inventor, mathematician, and physicist Galileo Galilei (1564–1642) was another central figure in the establishment of the

Galileo Galilei helped to establish science as we understand the term today. (Library of Congress, Prints and Photographs Division)

new sciences. Like Stevin, Galileo was introduced to mathematics fairly late in life. He received his early education at a monastery near Florence. Later he enrolled in the University of Pisa to study medicine. It was while he was a student at the University of Pisa that he overheard a geometry lesson. Until that time he had no exposure to mathematics. Though Galileo began his study of mathematics at the university, he eventually left because he did not have enough money for the fees. By the time of his departure, however, he was busy studying mathematics and physics. Soon he was teaching mathematics and publishing his discoveries in science. Like Stevin's, Galileo's work is characterized by rigorous mathematics and creatively designed and carefully conducted experiments.

Galileo is best known for the observations of the planets and stars that he made with the newly invented telescope and for the resulting persecution that he suffered at the hands of the Catholic Church. Galileo had apparently been sympathetic to Copernicus's ideas about the geometry of the solar system from the outset, but with his telescope he lifted the discussion out of the realm of theory and provided new and dramatic observations to support these ideas. His observations are carefully documented and analyzed in his letters and publications. Kepler was one of the people with whom Galileo corresponded. It is interesting that despite his contact with Kepler, Galileo, who in most respects was a revolutionary thinker, never did abandon the idea that the planets move in circular, rather than elliptical, orbits.

Galileo's work in science had great immediate impact, not only because some of his discoveries were dramatic, but also because he sought the attention. Unlike most of his contemporaries, who still followed the practice of publishing in Latin, Galileo published in Italian. He sought to attract the attention of the general public and to engage the public in the scientific controversies of the day. Furthermore, Galileo knew how to write. All of his scientific works were written with flair. He was not reluctant to respond to criticism or to criticize those with whom he disagreed. Sometimes he used reason, but he was not above using humor and sarcasm as well. His two major works, *Dialogue Concerning the Two Chief World Systems—Ptolemaic and Copernican* and *Dialogue Concerning Two New Sciences* (also known as *Two World Systems* and *Two New Sciences*, respectively), are important as literature and as science. They served to attract attention to the new ideas and to popularize them as well. Unlike many scientific treatises, Galileo's works generally sold well.

Galileo's book *Two New Sciences* is perhaps even more important than his writings about astronomy. In was through *Two New Sciences* that Galileo helped to invent and then popularize what has become "modern" science. Galileo wrote *Two New Sciences* late in life. He was already under house arrest for the views that he expressed in *Two World Systems*. (Galileo spent the last eight years of his life under house arrest.) As an additional condition of his punishment, he was ordered to cease writing about science during his incarceration. He wrote anyway. In addition to his isolation his writing difficulties were compounded by failing eyesight, which was perhaps the result of his telescopic observations of the Sun. When he completed the manuscript, he had it smuggled out and published in Leiden in 1638. This, too, was a dangerous action to take, given his relationship with the church. He died four years after the publication of *Two New Sciences*.

Two New Sciences is, like *Two World Systems*, written in the form of conversations among three characters. The conversations take place over the course of four days. Each day a different subject is discussed. There is also an appendix that contains some additional theorems on the centers of gravity of solids. Of special interest to us are the conversations that take place on the third and fourth days.

On the third day the characters discuss "naturally accelerated motion," or the motion of bodies undergoing constant acceleration. First, they discuss various experiments meant to illuminate certain aspects of naturally accelerated motion. The experimental results disprove various ideas about the motion of falling bodies that were then popular. They also serve to lead the reader to the ideas that Galileo thought true. After the experiments are discussed and the framework of the topic established, the main character of the story recites a long series of mathematical theorems and proofs regarding the nature of uniformly accelerated motion. These proofs rely heavily on classical Euclidean geometry. They demonstrate that each new result is a logical consequence of the previous ones, so if one accepts the previous ideas one must also accept these new, more sophisticated deductions as well. This collection of theorems and proofs shows just how proficient Galileo was at this type of mathematical reasoning. The combination of experimental results and mathematical analysis is exactly what distinguishes the "new sciences" from what preceded them.

In the section "Fourth Day" the characters consider projectile motion. Galileo is especially interested in explaining his ideas about the motion of a projectile that is thrown or fired on a trajectory that is initially horizontal. It is in this chapter that Galileo makes some of his most creative observations.

The structure of the chapter is essentially the same as that of the preceding chapter, except that this chapter begins with some geometric preliminaries. The characters begin by quoting the works of the great Greek geometers Apollonius and Euclid. Knowledge of Euclid's book *Elements* is clearly a prerequisite for the ensuing discussion. One of the characters even insists that "all real mathematicians assume on the part of the reader perfect familiarity with at least the *Elements* of Euclid."

After the lead character recalls for the reader some basic facts about Euclidean geometry, the three characters again discuss various experiments. These experiments are intended to elucidate the nature of projectile motion. In this section Galileo shows how creative a scientist he is by demonstrating how one can imagine the flight of a projectile as the combination of two motions. Each motion exists independently of the other. The first motion is a horizontal motion that continues at constant velocity. The second motion is a vertical motion that consists of a "naturally accelerated" motion, the subject of Galileo's previous chapter. Galileo's great insight is that projectile motion can be mathematically decomposed into a simple, uniform horizontal motion and the same type of vertical motion experienced by a body in free fall. This type of analysis, which is original with Galileo, is important because it is very useful. Galileo follows this analysis with a series of theorems and proofs about the properties of projectile

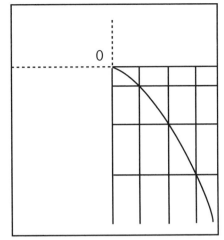

Galileo expressed his ideas about the motion of a projectile with a graph similar to this one. Suppose the projectile is fired at a horizontal trajectory from a cliff. The equally spaced vertical lines represent the x-coordinate of the projectile at equally spaced time intervals. The unequally spaced horizontal lines represent the y-coordinate of the projectile at equally spaced time intervals. The lines are unequal because the projectile is accelerating downward as a result of the force of gravity.

motion. In particular Galileo shows that in the absence of air resistance projectiles follow a parabolic path. (This is why he began with a discussion of Apollonius, the geometer in antiquity who made the greatest progress in understanding the properties of parabolas.)

Another important characteristic of Galileo's treatment of motion is that he clearly conceives of a force as something that changes a motion. This, too, is modern. He is less concerned with what a force is than with what it does, and over the course of the chapters "Third Day" and "Fourth Day," he describes what will later be known as Newton's first and second laws of motion.

Even today Galileo's discoveries are covered in any introductory physics course. Both his discoveries and his approach opened a new era in science. *Two New Sciences* was for its day a complete treatment of the problem of motion—not because Galileo solved all of the problems associated with motion, but because he solved most of the important problems that were solvable at the time. Galileo developed the conceptual framework necessary to investigate motion, but there were many problems that were out of his reach simply because he did not know sufficient math. Most problems associated with motion require quite a bit of mathematics for their solution. Most of the mathematics necessary to tackle these problems did not yet exist. In fact, a revolution in mathematics would have to occur before more complicated problems could be solved.

Fermat, Descartes, and Wallis

In the years following Galileo's death rapid strides were made in mechanics, the branch of physics concerned with forces, but progress in science sometimes depends on progress in mathematics. The problems with which these early scientists were concerned were often mathematically intractable given the state of mathematics at the time. Fortunately many of the best scientists of the time were also the best mathematicians, and rapid progress in science was accompanied by rapid progress in mathematics. During this period there were several important cases of independent discoveries of the same mathematical idea, and often a discovery in one field of mathematics contributed to the development of what (today) we would consider a separate branch of mathematics. Mathematics was assembling itself into a new and more powerful way of thinking than anything that had preceded it.

To appreciate the nature of some of the mathematical discoveries made during the latter half of the 17th century and the way they furthered humanity's understanding of the laws of nature, we need to keep in mind the type of mathematics that then existed. The mathematics of the Greeks and their Arabic and early Renaissance successors was fundamentally different from the mathematics that any high school student knows today. These early mathematicians, for example, had a very restricted knowledge of curves. The Greeks themselves were aware of only about a dozen curves, including the circle, the ellipse, the hyperbola, the parabola, and certain spirals. They had studied this small collection of curves to learn about their mathematical properties, but neither they nor their successors had found many uses for them. Nor had they developed general techniques for analyzing the curves that they did know. Probably they felt no need to develop more concepts because there were so few curves to analyze.

Conditions began to change during the Renaissance. Kepler discovered a use for the ellipse: Planetary orbits are elliptical. Galileo discovered a use for the parabola: In the absence of air resistance, a projectile follows a parabolic path. These were some of the very first uses of parabolas and ellipses discovered. Just as important many new curves were discovered during this time as well. Two of the most mathematically creative individuals of the time were the French philosopher, mathematician, and scientist René Descartes (1596–1650) and the French lawyer and mathematician Pierre de Fermat (1601–65).

Descartes and Fermat were both educated as lawyers. Descartes never worked as a lawyer. Fermat did legal work for his entire professional life. Fermat lived an ordered and genteel life in France. Descartes wandered about Europe for years. Fermat is best remembered for his mathematical contributions. Descartes, who was a creative mathematician and scientist, is today best remembered as a philosopher. Each found ways to relate algebraic equations to geometric curves. Each discovered that a single equation containing exactly two unknowns describes a curve, and each recognized the importance of this discovery. Once the connection between an equation and a curve was established, it was easy to generate numerous curves. As a result of the discovery of Descartes and Fermat, suddenly there were infinitely many different types of curves to study. The mathematical landscape had become far richer and new tools were required to analyze these curves.

Coordinate geometry was, in many ways, the key. Coordinate geometry allows the user to graph an equation. Throughout most of the history of mathematics, algebra and geometry had been separate disciplines. Coordinate geometry connected the two subjects. Insights into one branch of mathematics could be applied to problems in the other, and progress was greatly accelerated. The difficult geometric investigations favored by the Greeks had raised the level of rigor but had also in the end slowed progress. Algebra was replacing the awkward geometric analysis because it was often simpler to express the same idea using algebraic symbols than geometric diagrams. Using algebra was easier and more suggestive than using geometry. Algebra provided a language in which scientific and mathematical ideas could be more easily expressed. This capacity accelerated progress.

Descartes and Fermat studied more than curves; they began to study *tangents* to curves. (If we are given a curve and a point on a curve, the line tangent to the curve is the best straight-line approximation to the curve at the point.) The study of tangents was extremely important in the history of mathematics because knowing the slope of the line tangent to a curve at each point of a curve yields very specific information about the curve itself. (The slope of the tangent line is called the derivative.) For example, if we have an equation that describes the position of an object as a function of time, then the derivative, or slope of the tangent line, is the velocity at which the object is moving.

The computation of derivatives generally involves infinitesimal analysis, and Fermat, in particular, made a lot of progress in this area. It was he who developed the concept of a derivative. Another way of thinking about what a derivative means is that the derivative is a function that relates the rate of change of one vari-

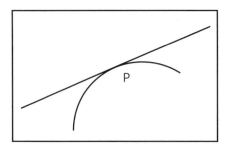

The line is tangent to the curve at the point P. At P the tangent line is the best straight-line approximation to the curve.

able as a function of another. Velocity, for example, is the rate of change of position with respect to time. Or to express this idea in another way: The derivative of the position of an object with respect to time is the velocity. Geometrically the derivative of a function at a point is just the slope of the tangent at that point. The discovery of the derivative and its meaning would have profound effects on the history of mathematics and science.

Fermat's research took him in still another direction. He was also interested in developing methods for computing the area beneath a curve. This idea also has important physical applications, and the techniques involved, as are those used for finding derivatives, depend on infinitesimal analysis. For example, if we have an equation that describes the velocity of an object as a function of time, then the area beneath the curve is the distance the object travels during the period of interest. Recall that this was Oresme's discovery, but Oresme knew only enough mathematics to examine the case of constant acceleration, which mathematically reduces to finding the area below a sloping line. Fermat went much further in his investigations and began to develop formulas for finding the area below a variety of curves. This concept and its associated techniques are called integration. The two concepts, differentiation and integration, make up the two halves of the subject that we now call calculus. Finding areas beneath curves involves the same sorts of infinite processes used by Archimedes and Stevin. The difference now is that the analysis is on a much higher level.

The third mathematician who contributed to this especially fertile time in mathematics history was the British mathematician John Wallis (1616–1703). Wallis developed an interest in mathematics after he was ordained a minister. There was civil war in England at the time. Both sides were engaged in the making and breaking of secret codes. It was during this time of war that the Reverend Wallis discovered he had a flair for cryptography. His skill at cryptography apparently sparked his interest in mathematics. Eventually Wallis moved to London and devoted his considerable intellect to the study of mathematics, a study that would occupy him for the rest of his life.

Wallis was an influential and prolific mathematician. He made three contributions that would prove to be particularly important to the development of laws of nature. First, Wallis contributed to the development of infinitesimal analysis. Many of his best discoveries in this regard are contained in his book *Arithmetica Infinitorum* (The arithmetic of infinitesimals). In this book he uses infinite processes to solve a great variety of problems. For example, one of his most famous discoveries is that the number $2/\pi$

equals the *infinite product* $\dfrac{1 \times 3 \times 3 \times 5 \times 5 \times 7 \times \ldots}{2 \times 2 \times 4 \times 4 \times 6 \times 6 \times \ldots}$. A more

modern way of saying the same thing is that the series of numbers

$\dfrac{1}{2}, \dfrac{1 \times 3}{2 \times 2}, \dfrac{1 \times 3 \times 3}{2 \times 2 \times 4}$ converges to the number $2/\pi$. Second, in

addition to his work with infinite products, Wallis, as Fermat did, also enjoyed solving problems in integration, such as finding the area beneath a curve, another application of infinitesimal analysis. His discoveries in this regard were important in themselves and inspired many mathematicians to improve and extend his results. Isaac Newton was one of the mathematicians inspired by Wallis's *Arithmetica Infinitorum.*

Finally, Wallis also made an important contribution to mechanics. His principal observation involved what scientists call momentum. Wallis examined the problem of colliding bodies and proposed the idea that momentum is conserved. To understand exactly what the words *momentum* and *conserved* means, it is helpful to know that some scientists in Wallis's time used the words *momentum* and *motion* interchangeably. We briefly adopt this archaic practice as we try to develop an appreciation of Wallis's insights. (Today scientists always make a distinction between motion and *momentum.*)

From the Renaissance onward scientists became increasingly quantitative in their outlook. They were no longer satisfied with qualitative questions and answers; they wanted numbers. So it was natural to begin to ask questions like, Which has more motion, a large ship traveling at few miles per hour or a bullet fired from the barrel of a gun? Of course the bullet has a much higher *velocity*, but in order to set a ship in motion a great deal more *mass* has to be moved. The answer to this and similar questions involving the relationships among mass, velocity, and motion lies in the definition of momentum, a definition that is familiar to all scientists today. *Both* the concepts of mass and of velocity come into play in the definition of momentum. The key, as Wallis well knew, is to define an object's momentum as the *product* of the object's mass and its velocity. The reason that the definition is so important is that momentum is an extremely important physical quantity.

Momentum is important because, as Wallis observed, it is a *conserved* quantity. To understand the meaning of the observation, suppose that we have two bodies that are in every way isolated from their surroundings. These two bodies form a system. To say that the system is isolated means that no outside forces act on the bodies, and that the two bodies exert no forces on the outside world; in this special case the only forces that act on the bodies are the forces that the bodies exert on each other. Though there are only two bodies in this simple illustration, there are three momenta to consider: the momentum of each individual body and the momentum of "the system," which consists of the sum of the momenta of the two bodies. This is called the total momentum. The momentum of the individual bodies can change. They may, for example, collide with each other. The collisions can consist of glancing blows or head-on crashes. The geometry of the collision has no effect on our considerations. Wallis's observation was that in the absence of outside forces *the total momentum of the system does not change*. In particular if as a result of a collision the momentum of one ball increases, the momentum of the second ball changes in such a way that *the sum of the two momenta is the same* as it was before the collision. When some property of an isolated system *cannot* change over time, then we say that that property is *conserved*. In this case if the momentum of the system is known at any point in time, then, as long as the system remains isolated from its surroundings, the momentum of the system

Descartes's conception of the universe as a system of vortices. This picture was first published in 1644. (Library of Congress, Prints and Photographs Division)

remains at that value for all time.

What has been said about a system of two bodies can also be said about an isolated system of many bodies. Suppose, for example, that we isolate many trillions of air molecules from their surroundings. This system is more complicated, but the molecules can still exert collision forces only on one another. Some of the collisions speed up individual molecules, some slow individual molecules down, and occasionally a collision occurs that causes one or more molecules to stop briefly. All of this happens in such a way that the total momentum of all the molecules remains constant.

Despite how modern much of the work of Wallis and the others sounds, the situation was actually somewhat more complicated. Descartes's ideas about the universe were very influential during this period. Everyone discussed in this chapter would have been familiar with them, and yet they are not in any way scientific. Descartes believed that the universe is filled with great vortices that carry the heavenly bodies along as they spin around each other (see the picture). His view would not fall out of fashion until Newton's ideas became known.

If we think of the science of motion as a puzzle, the scientists and mathematicians described in the chapter each solved a section of a very important puzzle. Galileo discovered a great deal about the science of motion, but his mathematics was not powerful enough to solve the problem. Descartes and Fermat discovered much of the mathematics necessary to express Galileo's insights in a way that would open them up to mathematical analysis. Wallis, who saw that momentum is conserved, had an important insight into nature. No one, however, had put all of these ideas and techniques together and used them to develop a sophisticated mathematical description, but that would happen soon enough.

5

MATHEMATICS AND THE LAW OF CONSERVATION OF MOMENTUM

It has often been said that the British physicist and mathematician Isaac Newton (1643–1727) was born the same day that Galileo died. It is a very poetic thought—the great Galileo's making way for the great Newton on the same day—but England and Italy were using different calendars at the time. When the same calendar is applied to both localities the remarkable coincidence disappears.

Galileo and Newton were two of the most prominent and best-known scientists of their respective generations. Their discoveries changed ideas about science and our place in the universe, but as individuals they had little in common:

- Galileo grew up with a freethinking, outspoken, creative father. Newton grew up without a father; his father died before he was born.

- Galileo published his ideas in Italian in an engaging literary style. Newton published his ideas in Latin, the language of the universities.

- Galileo did not shy away from controversy. In *The Assayer* Galileo mocks and satirizes his critics because they respond to his scientific discoveries by quoting Aristotle instead of attempting to verify the outcomes of his experiments and observations. Newton shunned controversy. While still a student at college Newton made many remarkable discoveries. But when he first published some of his ideas and they drew criticism, he retreated from the public eye for years.

- There were times when Newton had to be convinced by friends to publish his discoveries. Galileo, on the other hand, could not be prevented from publishing. Even under threat of imprisonment and worse, Galileo was irrepressible.

- Galileo remained actively involved in science until the end of his life. Newton largely ended his involvement with science and mathematics by the time he was middle-aged.

- Galileo was a social person who had a strong lifelong relationship with his daughter Virginia. Newton was a solitary, private person who spent much of his time researching alchemy.

Newton spent his earliest years with his mother, but when she remarried, he went to live with his grandmother. Later when his stepfather died, Newton returned to live with his mother. He was a quiet boy with a very active imagination. There are a number of stories about Newton's inventing various clever devices. In one in particular he frightens the people of the village where he lives by attaching a small lantern to a kite and using the kite to raise the lantern high over the village one evening.

Sir Isaac Newton expressed the science of motion via a set of axioms and theorems much as Euclid of Alexandria described geometry. (Library of Congress, Prints and Photographs Division)

As a young man Newton enrolled in Trinity College at the University of Cambridge. Newton's first interest was chemistry, but he soon began to read the most advanced mathematics and science books of his time. He began with a copy of Euclid's *Elements*. He read the works of the great French mathematician Viète. He read Kepler's writings on optics, as well as the works of Fermat and of Christian Huygens, the Dutch physicist and mathematician, and he was especially influenced by Wallis's book *Arithmetica Infinitorum*. He also read and was influenced by the writings of Galileo. During the next few years (1664–69) he made many of the discoveries for which he is remembered today.

One of Newton's earliest discoveries was the calculus. Calculus was the start of a new and important branch of mathematics called analysis. Mathematically calculus is usually divided into two separate branches. Both branches employ infinitesimal analysis. One branch of calculus focuses on derivatives, which relate the rate of change of the dependent variable to the independent variable. This branch of calculus, called the differential calculus, centers on two main questions: What are the mathematical techniques required to compute derivatives? How can derivatives be used to solve problems? The second part of calculus is called integral calculus. Initially integral calculus involved finding the area beneath a curve, sometimes called the integral of the curve, but the field soon grew to encompass a much larger class of problems. As differential calculus does, integral calculus centers on two questions: What are the mathematical techniques required to compute integrals? How can integrals be used to solve problems?

Even before Newton invented calculus, mathematicians had been busy answering these questions. Newton was not the first to compute integrals, nor was he the first to compute derivatives. Fermat was very adept at computing derivatives and knew how to compute a small number of integrals. He used these ideas and their associated techniques in his research. Similarly Wallis had learned to compute certain classes of integrals, so a great deal of the work involved in inventing calculus had already been done. Moreover, Newton, who was familiar with the work of Fermat and Wallis, could do all the problems that Fermat and Wallis had already solved, and he quickly learned to do more, but calculus involves more than these ideas and techniques.

Newton's great insight into calculus is that differentiation and integration are essentially *inverse operations* in the same way that addition and subtraction are inverse operations: Subtraction "undoes" the work of addition (and vice versa). Multiplication and division are also inverse to each other: Multiplication undoes the work of division (and vice versa). The relation between integration and differentiation is only slightly more complicated. Newton discovered that differentiation undoes the work of integration and that integration almost undoes the work of differentiation. To recover a function from its derivative we need to know a little more than its integral, but the additional difficulties involved are not great.

It is a simple matter to express Newton's observation that, mathematically speaking, differentiation and integration are two sides of the same coin symbolically. Suppose $p(x)$, which we just write as p, represents some function, and $\dot{p}$ is the derivative of p with respect to x. Recall that $\dot{p}$ tells us how p changes as x changes. Symbolically Newton discovered that if we know p, we can compute $\dot{p}$. The function $\dot{p}$ is called the derivative of p. Similarly if we know $\dot{p}$, we can (almost) compute p, where p is the integral of $\dot{p}$. Of course this simple notation belies the fact that difficult mathematics is often involved, but in principle the idea is easy. Differentiation undoes the work of integration and integration largely undoes the work of differentiation. This idea, which is called the fundamental theorem of calculus, was one of Newton's great discoveries.

One reason that Newton's discovery is so important is that it allows mathematicians to begin to solve equations when the derivative of a function is known but the function itself is unknown. The branch of mathematics concerned with identifying a function from information about its derivatives is called differential equations. In a differential equation, we are given information about the derivatives of a function, and our goal is to learn as much as possible about the function itself. The study of differential equations began as a part of calculus. Differential equations are extremely important in the history of mathematics and science, because the laws of nature are generally expressed in terms of differential equations. Differential equations are the means by which scientists describe and understand the world.

Newton's discovery of the fundamental theorem of calculus could have changed everything. He must have understood its importance, but his discovery had little immediate effect on his contemporaries because he did not publish it. The first person to discover calculus, including the relationship between a function and its derivatives, and to publish his ideas was Gottfried Wilhelm Leibniz (1646–1716).

Leibniz, who was born in Leipzig, was a prodigy. He entered university at Leipzig at age 15 and by age 17 earned a bachelor's degree. On his way to the doctorate he studied most of the subjects that the people of his time thought that a well-educated person requires: theology, law, philosophy, and mathematics. Leibniz was ready for a doctorate at age 20, and when the university declined to award it to him—they thought he was too young—he left to find a university more to his liking. He was soon awarded a doctorate of law at the University of Altdorf.

Today Leibniz is best remembered as a mathematician, but in his own time his interests and his activities were as broad as his education. There seemed few ideas that were beyond either his capacity or his interest. He invented a mechanical calculator. He contributed to the development of logic and algebra. He discovered the base 2 number system, which is very important in computers. He wrote about philosophy and religion and language, but he was not an academic in the usual sense. After he received his doctorate, Leibniz worked as a diplomat. He traveled widely. He maintained an active correspondence with the best mathematicians on the European continent, and in 1684 he began to publish his ideas on calculus. Though there is only one calculus—and so there is a lot of overlap in the ideas and concepts of Newton and Leibniz—there is little doubt that Leibniz was the better expositor. Leibniz enjoyed using language, verbal and written, and in his exposition of calculus he introduces a number of carefully thought-out, highly suggestive symbols. The symbols are chosen to reveal the concepts behind the ideas of calculus, and in large measure they work as he intended. Students have used Leibniz's mathematical notation as an aid in learning the calculus ever since. No one has ever claimed that Newton's notation could be used in the same way. Today all calculus texts employ Leibniz's notation.

The Laws of Motion

Newton's contributions to understanding the laws of nature, however, extended well beyond the invention of calculus, a mathematical language in which scientific ideas are readily expressed. Newton advanced several branches of science. The contribution of most interest to us is his mathematical study of motion. Newton's exposition of motion is classical in the sense that he

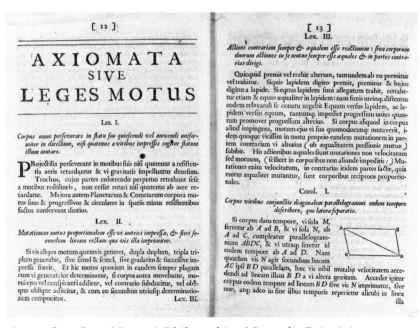

A page from Isaac Newton's Philosophiae Naturalis Principia Mathematica, *published in 1687. The three laws of motion shown here are the axioms of Newton's mathematical treatment of physics.* (Library of Congress, Prints and Photographs Division)

begins his presentation with a list of axioms and definitions. The emphasis on this axiomatic approach dates to the days of ancient Greece. It is the way Euclid began his work *Elements*. Axioms are the fundamental properties of the subject; they *define* the subject. They are, in a sense, the "rules of the game." From a logical point of view axioms are the ultimate reason that all subsequent deductions are true: The deductions are true because they are logical consequences of the axioms. Newton's axioms are called the laws of motion. Newton derives the properties of moving bodies as logical consequences of his axioms. As a consequence in every physical situation in which Newton's laws of motion are valid, so are all his conclusions, because his conclusions are mathematically derived from his laws of motion.

Recognizing the importance of his laws of motion, Newton lists them at the beginning of his work *Philosophiae Naturalis Principia Mathematica*, which is usually called *Principia*. He then begins deducing consequences of these laws in the form of mathematical theorems. Here are Newton's three laws in his own words:

1. Every body continues in its state of rest, or in uniform motion in a right line, unless it is compelled to change that state by forces impressed upon it.

2. The change of motion is proportional to the motive force impressed; and is made in the direction of the right line in which that force is impressed.

3. To every action there is always opposed an equal reaction; or, the mutual actions of two bodies upon each other are always directed to contrary parts.

> *(Newton, Isaac.* Mathematical Principles of Natural Philosophy. *Translated by Andrew Motte, revised by Florian Cajori.* Great Books of the Western World. *Vol. 16. Chicago: Encyclopaedia Britannica, 1952.)*

The first law states that in the absence of forces a body can be in one of two states. Either it is at rest (and remains at rest), or it moves at a constant velocity along a straight line (and continues to move in this way indefinitely). Newton refers to moving at constant speed along a straight line as "uniform motion in a right line." If an object is not moving at constant velocity along a right line—perhaps its velocity changes or its direction changes—then we can be sure that a force is acting on that body. More important and perhaps less obvious, in the first law Newton asserts that *only* forces change motions. Consequently motions and forces are very tightly linked.

Newton's second law is simply a description of *the ways* forces affect motions. Here Newton makes use of the vector property of a force, a property first described with precision by Simon Stevin. Every force has two properties, a strength and a direction. That is the reason for the semicolon in the second law. The part before the semicolon describes how the strength of the force affects the motion: If we double the force, we double the magnitude of the change. The second part of the second law—the part after the semicolon—relates the direction of the force to the direction of the change in motion: The change in direction of motion occurs on the line along which the force is applied.

The third law is bound up with the idea of conservation of momentum. Forces, according to Newton, occur in pairs. When one body exerts a force on a second body, the second body exerts a force on the first body. Newton also tells us how these two forces are related: They are equal in magnitude and opposite in direction. As a consequence when we add the two forces together they "cancel" each other, or add up to 0. Therefore in an isolated system, where the only forces exerted on two bodies are the forces that the bodies exert on each other, the total force on the system is 0, because the two equal and opposite forces cancel each other out. Given that *only* forces can change motions—that is the content of first law—and that the total force on the system is 0, the momentum of the system *cannot change*. This is evidently Wallis's insight, too, but Newton's third law is in a form that is more amenable to mathematical analysis. (Of course these qualities are not exclusive to two bodies in motion. What has been said for two bodies in motion also holds true for a larger, more complicated system of bodies.)

It was the mathematical expression of Newton's three laws that made a profound and permanent change in science and technology. Expressing the laws of motion mathematically involves calculus. Mathematically we can say that *the time rate of change in momentum equals the sum of the forces.* In other words if we know the forces acting on a body, we also know the *derivative* of the momentum. If we know the derivative of the momentum then we can integrate it to find the momentum itself. With the help of Newton's three laws and calculus it is possible to compute not just the current momentum of the body but the momentum of the body in the future and in the past as well. Newton's work enabled scientists to *predict* the motion of objects by using very general principles. With additional work it is even possible to use Newton's laws and calculus to compute the *position* of the body both in the past and in the future. That is why applying calculus to the laws of motion made such a huge difference in the history of science. After Newton's work established these principles, computing the momentum and the position of an object once the forces acting on the object were established was possible.

The mathematical expression of Newton's idea is deceptively simple. Traditionally the momentum of a body is often represented with the letter p, and p is a function of time. If we use Newton's calculus notation, then the rate of change of p with respect to time is denoted by $\dot{p}$. Symbolically Newton's laws assert that $\dot{p}$ equals the sum of the forces acting on the body. Let $F_1, F_2, F_3, \ldots, + F^n$, represent a complete list of all the forces acting on a body and let p represent the body's momentum. Newton's laws of motion are summed up in the equation $\dot{p} = F_1 + F_2 + F_3 + \ldots + F^n$, but we can make the equation even simpler. We can use Stevin's discovery about how to combine all of the forces that appear on the right side of the equation. If we let the letter F represent the sum of all the forces, then Newton's laws of motion can be expressed in the extremely simple-looking equation $\dot{p} = F$. The point is that if we can *measure* F and we know p for even one instant of time, then we can *compute* p for all time. During Newton's life this discovery had its greatest expression when F represented the force of gravity.

Newton also discovered the so-called law of gravity. The law of gravity is a statement about the nature of the force of gravity. It describes how the strength and direction of the force of gravity exerted by two bodies on each other change as the distance between the bodies changes. In our notation Newton discovered a formula for the force F that appears in the equation $\dot{p} = F$. Notice that if he knows F, where F now represents the force of gravity, then he knows $\dot{p}$, the derivative of the momentum. Next, using calculus, Newton was able to compute the momentum and then use this information to compute the path that each planet takes as it orbits the Sun. What he discovered is that his computed paths were in close agreement with those that Kepler had worked out by analyzing Tycho Brahe's data. This is a powerful indicator that Newton had gotten it right.

The equation $\dot{p} = F$ has uses in addition to predicting the orbital paths of planets. It describes an extremely strong limitation on the motion of any body. The restriction is that the derivative of the momentum of the body *must equal* the sum of the forces acting on it. Any other possibility is not "physical"—another way of saying that it just cannot happen. Scientists have used Newton's laws ever since in the description of the motions of everything from rockets to oceans.

It may seem that this relationship solves the problem of how bodies move, and in theory it almost does. The last difficulty arises when we try to compute the momentum from the equation $\dot{p} = F$. To complete the computation we need one more bit of information. To see the problem, imagine that we are in a car moving down a highway at constant velocity. It is easy to predict our location at the end of an hour provided we know our location at the beginning of the hour. A problem arises, however, when we do not know our initial location with precision. In this case we cannot predict our final location with certainty, although we can still predict how far we will have traveled over the course of the hour. This is the difficulty alluded to earlier in the chapter when we mentioned that the relationship between integration and differentiation is *almost* analogous to the relationship between addition and subtraction or multiplication and division. To compute a function from its derivative we need one extra bit of information. In our example the other bit corresponds to knowing our initial position. More generally to solve the equation $\dot{p} = F$ completely, that is, to find the momentum of the object for every point in time, we need to know the momentum of the object at any one point in time. If we know this, then we can compute the momentum of the object for *all* time. Practically speaking this last bit of information, the bit needed to find the momentum function from Newton's equation of motion, is usually obtained by making a measurement. Measurements generally involve some uncertainty, and as a consequence there is always some uncertainty about the computed momentum as well. As a general rule, however, the problem is not great in the sense that if a small error is made in the measurement, the answer we compute contains only a small error as well.

The effect of Newton's work cannot be overestimated. Conservation of momentum is the first major conservation law of classical physics. Newton's discoveries make many important phenomena in physics predictable. In other words if we are given a body and the forces acting on the body, then it is possible to calculate a unique solution, and *that solution must describe the motion of the body*. Newton's laws and calculus make it possible to treat motion as a series of causes and effects: The cause of the change in motion is the applied force. The effect is the new (computed) motion. This is an extraordinary insight into the workings of nature.

The Discovery of Neptune

Newton's analysis of planetary motion was in good agreement with that of Kepler, and this agreement was taken as evidence that Newton's mathematical model is a good reflection of reality. What scientists of the time did not know is that there are small but measurable differences between the motion of the planets as predicted by Newton's and Kepler's models and the measurements of the actual positions of the planets. The difficulty arises because Newton's model does not—and Kepler's model cannot—take into account the gravitational interactions that occur between the planets themselves.

The gravitational field of the Sun is so much stronger than that of any planet that every planet moves almost as if the only force affecting its motion is that of the Sun. That is why when Newton computed the motion of each planet under the gravitational pull of the Sun, the results he obtained were very close to the phenomena that had been observed. As increasingly accurate measurements accumulated, however, scientists sought a model that would account for the small differences between what they observed and what they calculated. These small differences, called perturbations, are due to the gravitational interactions that occur between the planets themselves. Developing a model to account for these small planet-to-planet interactions was a major goal of those who worked after Newton, and the first to succeed was the French mathematician and scientist Pierre-Simon Laplace (1749–1827).

Laplace was one of the major scientific and mathematical figures of his time. His ideas influenced the development of the theory of probability for much of the 19th century, for example, and his accomplishments in astronomy had a profound effect on those who followed him. Laplace's best-known achievement in astronomy involved developing a sophisticated mathematical model of planetary motion, a model so powerful that he was able to compute the perturbations in the orbit of one planet that are due to its gravitational interaction with other planets. This is a difficult mathematical problem because the effect of one planet on the orbit of its neighbors depends on the relative positions of the planets, and, of course, their relative positions are continually changing. Laplace's work did more than provide a basis for accurate calculations, however.

At this time there was also discussion among astronomers about whether the solar system is stable; that is, they wanted to know whether the cumulative effect of all of these planet-to-planet interactions would not eventually disrupt the solar system. Because the effect of one planet on another is to change both its speed and its direction, it seemed at least possible that over time the planets would be pulled out of their orbits and the solar system would collapse into chaos. Laplace was able to show that this could not occur. The solar system will maintain its present configuration into the indefinite future. The solar system is stable. This, too, was an important scientific accomplishment. It was so important and so impressive that at first it seemed that Laplace had solved the last big problem in predicting planetary motions, but a new and even more difficult problem was already on the horizon.

In 1781 the German-born British astronomer and musician William Herschel (1738–1822) discovered the planet Uranus. Herschel was not the first person to observe Uranus. As a naked-eye object Uranus is very dim when viewed from Earth. It is right at the limit of what can be seen with the naked eye, so even a small telescope reveals its presence, but Herschel was the first to notice its exceptional appearance. Further observation proved that it was a planet.

Uranus was the first planet to be discovered in recorded history, and its discovery caused quite a sensation. Astronomers immediately began to measure its motion across the night sky, because once they knew how long Uranus took to orbit the Sun they could, with the help of Kepler's laws of planetary motion, compute its approximate distance from the Sun. They discovered that, by the standards of the time, Uranus is almost unimaginably far away (2.9 billion km or 1.8 billion miles).

Having established its approximate distance, astronomers next attempted to compute its future positions in the night sky. This can be done by using Newton's laws of motion, calculus, and the law of gravity. Thanks to Newton's work on gravity and Laplace's extension of Newton's work, these astronomers knew the forces acting on Uranus that were due to the Sun, Saturn, and Jupiter. They could compute the effect of these forces on the motion of Uranus. They were surprised, therefore, when the orbital motion that they measured was not the same one that they computed.

There was more than one explanation for Uranus's unpredictable motion, and each explanation had its adherents. One explanation was that the measurements were inaccurate, but as more and more measurements accumulated, this hypothesis fell out of favor. Another explanation for the discrepancy between the observed motion and the predicted motion was that Newton's laws of motion might not be valid at such a great distance from Earth. Newton's laws had been thought to be invariant with respect to position; that is another way of saying that the change of a given body in response to a given set of forces should not depend on where the body is located. There was, of course, no way for anyone to be certain that Newton's laws remained valid so far from Earth, but aside from Uranus's anomalous motion, there was no reason to suspect that the laws also did not hold in the vicinity of Uranus. Whatever the cause the difference between their computed predictions of Uranus's position in the night sky and their measurements were too big to ignore. Could it be that Newton, Laplace, and others had overlooked something?

A third explanation, which was based on the assumption that Newton was correct, was proposed: Recall that Newton's equation of motion is a mathematical statement that the change of momentum of a body equals the *sum* of the forces acting on the body. In other words, in order to compute Uranus's momentum as well as its position, one needed to know all the forces acting on Uranus. If there was an unknown force acting on Uranus, this might account for the difference between its observed and its predicted positions.

The British mathematician and astronomer John Couch Adams (1819–92) and the French mathematician and astronomer Urbain-Jean-Joseph Le Verrier (1811–77) independently concluded that there is another force affecting Uranus's motion through space. They believed that this additional force was the gravitational attraction of still another undiscovered planet. Adams was the first to draw this conclusion, and he began to try to compute the position of the unseen planet. A few years later Le Verrier began to try the same thing. Trying to compute the position of an unseen object from the gravitational effects that it exerts on another body is a very difficult mathematics problem to solve. In fact many people who believed in the possibility of an undiscovered planet never tried to compute the position of the unknown planet. The computational difficulties seemed insurmountable.

Adams worked on the problem off and on for five years; Le Verrier worked on it for two years. Until recently historians had always believed that they finished at about the same time and with essentially the same answer. What is certain is that it was Le Verrier's calculations that were experimentally verified. Le Verrier found an observatory that would scan the sky for a new planet at the location that he predicted. The observatory took less than an hour to find Neptune. It was located within 1° of Le Verrier's computed position. (In 1999 long-lost historical documents uncovered in Chile indicated that Adams had not progressed as far in the computation of Neptune's position as was previously believed. His computations were far less accurate than Le Verrier's, and he was far less certain about Neptune's position. In retrospect it was really only Le Verrier who discovered Neptune.)

The discovery of Neptune was hailed as one of the great scientific triumphs of the 19th century. Galileo, Newton, Laplace, and others had developed a new way of understanding nature. With the help of new mathematical and scientific insights scientists were no longer simply looking for patterns; they were predicting them. Given a cause, scientists had learned to predict an effect. Given an effect, Le Verrier had discovered the cause. The principle of the conservation of momentum, measurements of Uranus's motion, and a great deal of mathematics enabled Le Verrier to show that it was possible to discover a new world without ever looking through a telescope.

6

MATHEMATICS
AND THE LAW OF
CONSERVATION OF MASS

Another important early conservation law concerns not motion, but matter. The law of conservation of mass was first established by the French chemist and government official Antoine-Laurent Lavoisier (1743–94). Lavoisier lived in turbulent times. As were those of many French mathematicians and scientists whose stories are detailed in other volumes of this series, Lavoisier's life and work were influenced by political turbulence in his native country. For Lavoisier the results were tragic.

Lavoisier was born into comfortable surroundings. His mother died when he was young and he was raised by his father and grandmother. As a youth he showed an early interest in and aptitude for science. His father, a well-placed government official, ensured that his son received an excellent education. Lavoisier studied a wide variety of subjects at Collège Mazarin—languages, mathematics, chemistry, astronomy, literature, and philosophy were some of the fields in which he received instruction—and while in college distinguished himself in several areas. For example he won awards for rhetoric and for his translations of Greek to French. He studied law at the Sorbonne and received a license to practice law, but from the beginning clearly his main interest was science.

After receiving his license to practice law, Lavoisier began his study of science. He wrote a paper on how to light a large town, a paper that won him an award from the Academy of Sciences. He wrote about aurorae, thunder, chemical analysis, and geology. His methods are marked by carefully designed, carefully conducted experiments that yielded quantitative rather than just qualitative results. His papers show how meticulously he made measurements at each step of an experiment and how aware he was of any possible sources of error in his work. In many ways his papers have a modern feel to them.

Lavoisier's approach was new for the time and his work helped initiate what is sometimes called the chemical revolution. He was especially interested in the problem of combustion, and he investigated the role of air in combustion. (To appreciate the difficulties involved keep in mind that in Lavoisier's time there was no real understanding of the chemical composition of air or of the process of combustion. Today we know that air is mostly nitrogen and that it is only the approximately 20 percent of air that is oxygen that sustains a combustion reaction. We also know that oxygen is not "consumed" in combustion but rather combined with other elements, usually carbon or hydrogen, to form new compounds. Lavoisier had to work out the general outlines of this process for himself.)

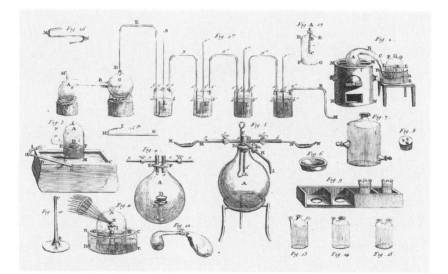

Scientific equipment from the laboratory of Antoine-Laurent Lavoisier (Library of Congress, Prints and Photographs Division)

Lavoisier distinguished between chemical elements and compounds. Elements, he said, are substances that cannot be broken down. He began to classify substances as compounds or elements. His discoveries led to a new way of perceiving nature. His insightful experiments, his personal prestige, and his numerous well-written accounts of his results were important in spreading the new ideas. Within Lavoisier's lifetime many scientists accepted his concepts and rejected the idea, which dated back to ancient Greece, that there are four elements: earth, air, fire, and water.

As Lavoisier rose to prominence he became actively involved in governmental affairs: collection of taxes, finance, agriculture, education, and other areas. Some of these activities benefited the general public. Some, such as tax collection, benefited the monarchy and aroused public wrath. He helped to establish savings banks and insurance societies, and he helped to promote public hygiene. In the end, however, Lavoisier's contemporaries recalled only his association with the tax collection agency.

With the French Revolution, power seemed to have been transferred from the monarchy and toward more democratic institutions. Lavoisier initially supported the French Revolution, but his association with the tax collection agency made him a target of political reprisals among the more radical revolutionaries. By 1793 the ideals of the revolution had been subverted and the so-called Reign of Terror had begun. By 1794 Lavoisier and other officials associated with the collection of taxes were rounded up, subjected to a brief mass trial, and executed. Lavoisier was among 28 former tax officials who were killed on May 8, 1794.

After his tragic death Lavoisier's ideas continued to spread among scientists. In fact his stature as a scientist seemed to grow. Especially important was Lavoisier's view that the common measure of matter is weight. (Recall that Leonardo's version of a conservation law used volume as a measure of the amount of matter flowing past a point.) Because liquid water is nearly incompressible, whether water is measured by volume or by mass is fairly unimportant, but the situation is different for gases. Gases may expand or contract a lot, depending on changes in the gas temperature and pressure. Consequently Lavoisier needed a better measure of the amount of matter in a sample than its volume. At Earth's surface weight is a more fundamental measure. This concept, too, is almost modern. Today scientists use mass as a measure of the quantity of matter in a body, but at Earth's surface mass and weight are proportional. This means that at Earth's surface there is a simple relationship between mass and weight. As a consequence if we can measure the weight we can compute the mass.

Throughout his career as a scientist Lavoisier performed numerous experiments in which he measured the weight of the reactants, which are the materials present before the reaction, and the products, which are the materials produced by the reaction. As his experimental techniques improved he was able to show that the difference in weight between the products and the reactants was always small. The question that he had to decide was whether the difference in weight between the products and reactants that he seemed to detect almost every time he performed an experiment was due to small inaccuracies in measurement or to the creation or destruction of matter. When we are taught science, we begin with the assumption that matter is neither created nor destroyed in chemical reactions; Lavoisier, by contrast, had to establish this fact.

Lavoisier developed a model in which chemical reactions involve the modification of matter but not its destruction or creation, where we take weight to be the measure of matter. He was right, of course, and his insight led to a new conservation law. One way of formulating his idea is to say that in a system isolated from its surroundings the mass of the system is constant. If we use Newton's notation, we can write a mathematical formulation of the preceding sentence, $\dot{m} = 0$, where m represents the amount of mass in the system and the dot represents the rate of change with respect to time. More generally when the system is not isolated from its surroundings, we say that the change in the mass of the system is the difference between the mass that moves into the system and the mass that moves out, or $\dot{m} = m_{in} - m_{out}$.

This equation represents a very powerful constraint on the way the mass of the system can change. It says that to keep track of the change of mass inside the system we need only make measurements along the boundary, because only there can mass enter or leave the system. Furthermore any function that we claim describes the amount of mass in the system must have the property that the derivative of the function—that is, the rate of change of our mass function per unit of time—must satisfy this differential equation. Finally, in the same way that we can solve a differential equation for the momentum of a system, we can solve the differential equation for the mass of the system.

Physical systems that can be described by these types of differential equations are deterministic. In particular if we know the forces acting on the system and the mass flow into and out of the system (and if we know the state of the system at one instant of time), we can compute the mass and momentum of the system for some later time. The effect of these two conservation laws on the development of science and technology was profound.

Leonhard Euler and the Science of Fluid Dynamics

One of the first people to use the laws of conservation of mass and conservation of momentum simultaneously in the study of a single phenomenon was the Swiss mathematician Leonhard Euler (1707–83). He was the first mathematician to produce a set of differential equations that describe the motion of a particular type of fluid. Euler was probably the most prolific mathematician of all time, and there were very few areas of mathematics that existed during his life to which he did not contribute.

As a young man Euler attended the University of Basel, where he studied theology as well as medicine, languages, mathematics, physics, and astronomy. His primary interest, however, was always mathematics. Euler is said to have been able to compose mathematics papers in his head in the same way that it is said that Mozart could compose music: prolifically and without hesitation. During the last 17 years of his life Euler was blind, but during this period his mathematical output only increased.

With respect to the science of fluids Euler proposed a set of differential equations that describe the motion of a particular type of fluid. He was the first to do this. The set he chose consists of specialized versions of the conservation of mass and

The motion of the atmosphere is extremely complex and results in beautiful and unexpected patterns. The motion of air is one of the most important phenomena modeled by fluid dynamics equations. (Courtesy of National Oceanic and Atmospheric Administration/Department of Commerce)

conservation of momentum equations—versions that he created to describe a particular type of fluid. The assumptions on which the equations are based are comparable to axioms. In this sense Euler did for fluid dynamics what Euclid did for geometry and what Newton did for the motion of rigid bodies. If one accepts Euler's assumptions—expressed as they are in a system of equations—then one must also accept the conclusions derived from the equations, and the conclusions derived from the equations *are* the solutions to the equations. Euler's great innovation was to demonstrate that it was possible to turn the science of fluids into a deductive discipline. By creating these equations, Euler demonstrated the feasibility of studying fluids mathematically.

Euler's equations are still used today, but they do not describe the way every fluid moves in response to forces. No one set of equations can do that, because every set of equations incorporates certain facts and/or opinions about the physical properties of the fluid under consideration. Euler's equations have been successfully used to model the motion of various fluids—liquids as well as gases—provided the physical properties of the fluids satisfy certain very narrow technical criteria. Most fluids do not meet Euler's criteria, however. When the criteria are not satisfied, one can in theory still solve the equations, but the solutions have no physical meaning. This is where science—as well as mathematics—comes into play. The researcher must strike a balance between a set of

THE MATHEMATICS OF COMBUSTION

Our society is founded on combustion technology. Almost all transportation vehicles in use today rely on the internal combustion engine. In terms of transportation we cannot do without it. Although there is a greater mix of technologies in the area of electrical power generation—some power is produced by nuclear and hydroelectric power plants as well as very small amounts of "alternative" power sources—combustion technology is a vital, and for now, an irreplaceable part of our power generation system. In cold climates combustion of gas, oil, wood, or coal prevents many people from freezing during the winter. Combustion technology is everywhere.

In addition to making our way of life possible, combustion reactions are a major source of pollution. The chemical characteristics of the atmosphere as well as those of many freshwater lakes and rivers are being slowly altered by the by-products of the combustion reactions that our houses, cars, planes, ships, factories, and power plants release into

Test firing of the Saturn rocket engine, an especially dramatic form of combustion (Courtesy of National Aeronautics and Space Administration)

(continues)

THE MATHEMATICS OF COMBUSTION
(continued)

the air. Both the benefits and the drawbacks of combustion reactions have led to enormous amounts of research into the mechanical and chemical characteristics of combustion.

The processes that occur in real combustion reactions are exceedingly complex. One commonly studied reaction occurs when the fuel and air are premixed to form a highly combustible mixture. As part of the mixture burns, the surrounding medium is heated by the burning and becomes more buoyant than the mixture above it. It begins to rise (Archimedes' buoyancy principle). The rising gases acquire momentum (Newton's laws of motion). As the fuel-air mixture passes through the flame front, the chemical composition of the mixture is changed and heat is released. The chemical composition of the reacting chemicals must change in such a way that mass is conserved (conservation of mass). The large rapid changes in the temperature of the reactants that are typical of most combustion reactions cause the resulting motions of the gases to become turbulent and chaotic. There are many interesting and surprising phenomena that occur inside a fire or explosion.

Mathematical models for such complicated phenomena frequently give rise to very complicated sets of equations. There are separate equations for mass, momentum, and energy as well as equations that describe the precise chemical reactions, and these equations are generally *coupled*. This means that it is not possible to solve them one at a time, because the solution of one equation depends on the solution of other equations. As a consequence all of the equations must be solved simultaneously. Even the fastest computers do not readily produce accurate solutions to these equations. Combustion modeling remains a very active area of scientific research.

equations that accurately reflect the physical properties of the fluid and a set of equations that are still simple enough to solve. Usually what the researcher gains in one area is lost in the other. Striking a balance requires experience and insight.

In practice, the principal difficulty with Euler's approach is that the resulting equations are usually always very difficult to solve. The existence of intractable problems is characteristic of the field of fluid dynamics. They arise because under the action of a force a fluid deforms continuously. When one region of the fluid begins to flow, that motion is transmitted to other parts of the fluid, and soon the entire mass begins to swirl around. This coupling of the motion in one part of a fluid with motions in other parts causes complex, beautiful, and often surprising patterns of flow.

The development of computers has been a great help in understanding some of the properties of the solutions of equations of fluid dynamics, but computational solutions leave many problems unresolved as well. For example, the fact that the computer can find *a* solution is no guarantee that another solution does not exist for the same situation. It may be that one set of equations has multiple solutions for the same "input." The existence of multiple solutions is critical, because if other, different solutions exist for the same set of conditions, then predicting the behavior of the fluid becomes much more difficult. This is one reason that there are still many mathematicians who devote their time to studying very basic, noncomputational questions about the nature of the equations that arise in the study of fluids. Euler founded the science of mathematical fluid dynamics, but his main contribution lies in the statement of the problem rather than in any solutions that he found.

7

MATHEMATICS AND THE LAWS OF THERMODYNAMICS

Thermodynamics is that branch of science that deals with the relationships that exist between heat and work. In a practical sense thermodynamics is concerned with our ability to turn heat energy into electrical energy, as is done at oil, coal, gas, and nuclear power plants. It is also concerned with the problem of turning heat energy into the energy of motion, as in cars, ships, and planes. But thermodynamics also has a theoretical side. Theoretically thermodynamics is concerned with energy, work, and the concept of irreversibility. (A process is irreversible if it cannot be undone; combustion, for example, is an irreversible process.) More than most branches of science thermodynamics is also a subject that has inspired a great deal of philosophical speculation. It touches on important questions about why physical systems evolve in some ways but not others. It is one of the conceptually richest areas of classical physics.

The history of thermodynamics traces its roots to experiments performed by the Italian physicist and mathematician Galileo Galilei. Galileo is often given credit for being the first to devise a thermometer. In the study of heat a thermometer is a valuable tool. It enables the user to measure changes in temperature and to compare the temperature of various objects and materials by "taking" their temperatures. Galileo's invention was an important innovation because two objects at the same temperature often *feel* as if they are at different temperatures. For example, if we touch a slab of wood and a slab of iron, both of which are at room temperature, the iron feels cooler. Thermometers provide an objective way of comparing temperatures, but they do not offer much insight into what temperature is.

The study of thermodynamics began in earnest with the work of the French-born British inventor and scientist Denis Papin (1647–1712). Papin was well connected; he had already worked with the Dutch physicist, mathematician, and inventor Christian Huygens and the British physicist Robert Boyle before he began to think about steam. Papin invented what he called a "digester," which is what we would call a pressure cooker. The goal is to turn water to steam in a sealed container. The result is that pressure in the container quickly increases. The boiling temperature of the water also rapidly increases. Pressure cookers are useful devices for cooking food provided the containers do not explode. Papin's solution to the problem of exploding containers was to design a safety valve. When the pressure increased enough, it raised the valve and released some of the pressure. It was Papin's insight that the pressure that the steam exerted on the safety valve might also

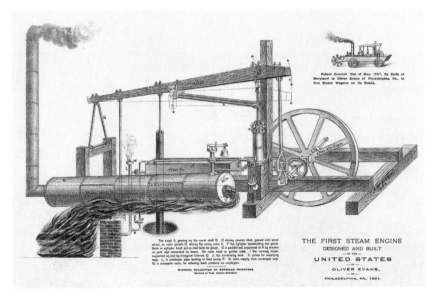

The first steam engine designed and built in the United States, 1801
(Library of Congress, Prints and Photographs Division)

drive a piston. As the piston rose it could be made to raise a weight or do other useful work.

Papin's idea of driving a piston with steam was soon incorporated into a practical steam-driven pump by the British inventor Thomas Savery (ca. 1650–1715). Savery received the first patent for a steam-driven pump, which was used to remove water from mines. Savery's design was crude but it was soon improved. Savery formed a partnership with another British inventor, Thomas Newcomen (1663–1729). The new engine that resulted from the partnership, designed by Newcomen, was a substantial improvement, but it was still very wasteful of energy.

Fortunately one of Newcomen's engines broke and was taken to a little-known repairman named James Watt (1736–1819). While repairing the Newcomen engine, Watt saw a way that the efficiency of the engine could be substantially improved. In 1769 James Watt applied for his first steam engine patent. It was the first of many patents that Watt received for improving the steam engine. By the time he had finished his work on the steam engine, Watt's engines were installed in mines and factories throughout Britain, and Watt had become a wealthy and celebrated man. The British Industrial Revolution was now in full swing, and it was powered by the Watt steam engine. The race to understand the relationship between heat and work had begun.

Steam engines are heat engines. Anyone wishing to understand the physical principles on which a steam engine is based must also understand heat. James Watt's friend and financial backer the British chemist, physician, and physicist Joseph Black (1728–99) was one of the first to make a serious attempt to understand the nature of heat.

Black had received a very broad education at Glasgow University, where he studied medicine and science, and at the University of Edinburgh, where he studied medicine. Black later taught chemistry, anatomy, and medicine at the University of Glasgow. He was also a practicing physician, but today he is remembered for his work in chemistry and physics. In chemistry he showed that the colorless, odorless gas carbon dioxide is a gas different from ordinary air; these experiments preceded those of

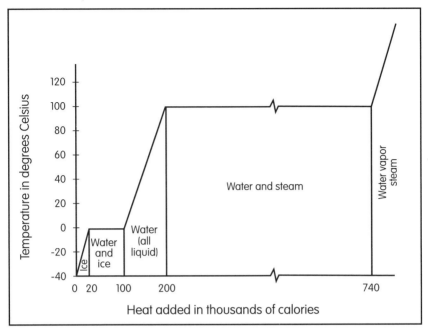

Heat is steadily added to a block of ice initially at −40°C:
1. First the ice warms until it reaches the melting point (sensible heat).
2. Additional heat causes the ice to melt but does not cause a change in temperature (latent heat).
3. Once the ice has melted the temperature increases steadily until the boiling point is reached (sensible heat).
4. The water boils with no change in temperature (latent heat).
5. When the water has turned to vapor, the temperature again begins to increase (sensible heat).

Lavoisier. In physics Black undertook one of the first serious studies of the nature of heat. His experiments with heat and his theory of heat are his most important contributions to the history of the science of thermodynamics.

Black noticed several important properties of heat. He noticed that the addition of heat to a body sometimes raises the temperature of the body, but sometimes heat can be added to a body without raising its temperature. For example, if heat is added to a container of cool water, the water responds with an increase in temperature. If, however, the water is already boiling, increasing the rate at which heat is added simply causes the water to boil faster; the temperature of the water does not change. Similarly adding heat to a block of ice causes the temperature of the ice to increase until it is at the temperature at which ice melts (32°F or 0°C). If additional heat is transferred while the ice is at the melting point, the ice melts, but its temperature does not increase until all the ice has turned to water.

The change of any substance from vapor to liquid, or liquid to vapor, or the change of any substance from liquid to solid, or solid to liquid, is a *phase change*. (Matter generally exists in one of three phases: vapor, liquid, or solid.) Black's experiments showed that when a material undergoes a phase change, the temperature remains constant until the phase change is complete. Black responded to these observations by defining heat in terms of what it does rather than what it is. He called heat that causes a change in temperature *sensible heat*. He called heat that causes a change of phase *latent heat*.

Black also noticed variations in what we now call the specific heat of bodies. To understand the idea, imagine that we transfer the same amount of heat to two liquids of identical mass. We may, for example, use water and ethyl alcohol. Though the amount of heat transferred to each body is the same, the resulting change in temperature is different: The temperature of the alcohol increases more than the temperature of the water. Furthermore not only does the change in temperature vary with the material; so does the amount of expansion or contraction as heat moves into or out of the material. For Black and his contemporaries the complex interactions that they observed between heat and matter were a barrier to understanding the nature of heat.

After he had developed a significant body of experimental results, Black created what he called the caloric theory to explain what he had observed. Caloric, he hypothesized, is a fluid that can flow from one body to another. When a warm body is placed in contact with a cool body, caloric flows out of the warm body into the cool one. The temperature of the warm body diminishes as the temperature of the cool body increases. Furthermore as caloric flows from one body to the other, the volume of the warm body diminishes and the volume of the cool body increases. Having hypothesized the existence of caloric, he was able to deduce various properties that it must have in order to make his theory consistent. The most important of these properties was that caloric is conserved; that is, Black's idea was that caloric, as well as momentum and mass, cannot be created or destroyed. Black had proposed a new conservation law.

In retrospect seeing why Black believed caloric was conserved is easy: Experiments had enabled him to determine how much of an increase in caloric (heat) is needed to raise the temperature of a particular body a given number of degrees. He was also able to measure how much of a decrease in caloric is necessary to lower the temperature of that same body a given number of degrees. When he placed two bodies in contact with each other, he could compute the amount of caloric that flowed out of one body into the other by taking the temperature of only one of the bodies. This enabled him to compute the temperature change in the second body: A decrease in caloric in the first body is reflected in an increase in caloric in the second body. These findings led Black to conclude that caloric is being neither created nor destroyed; it is simply being transferred from one body to another.

Black's conservation of caloric law was very influential. Many of the best scientists of the day accepted it, but from the start there were some dissenters as well. An early voice of dissent was that of the American-born physicist, inventor, and administrator Benjamin Thompson (1753–1814), also known as Count Rumford. Thompson was a British loyalist during the American Revolutionary War. He served as a British spy for part of the war and later served as a British officer in New York. At the conclusion of the war he wisely moved to Britain.

Thompson had a highly inventive mind. He lived for a time in England and later moved to Bavaria. While there he invented the drip coffeepot and a type of kitchen range. He improved the design of fireplaces and chimneys. As an administrator in Bavaria he introduced a number of social reforms and helped James Watt's steam engine to gain wide use. Most important for the history of science, as director of the Bavarian arsenal Thompson supervised the boring of cannons. The boring of cannons is slow, hot work. As the drill cuts into the metal, it produces many small metal chips. The temperatures of the bit and the cannon soar. Water is poured onto the bit to prevent both the bit and the cannon from overheating, but the water must be continually replenished because it boils off.

According to the caloric theory the enormous amount of heat that is generated by the process is due to the chips that are produced during drilling. The small chips cannot hold as much heat as the large cylinder from which they are cut. As a consequence caloric flows out of the chips into the water and causes it to boil. The boiling water is simply a consequence of the conservation of caloric. What Thompson noticed, however, is that after a drill bit is run for a while it becomes so dull that it no longer cuts into the metal. As a consequence no metal chips are produced. But still the water that is poured onto the dull bit boils: The bit is hot, the cannon metal is hot, and the water is hot. Thompson concluded that the friction of the dull bit on the cannon was *creating* caloric. This showed (according to Thompson) that caloric is not being conserved. Thompson even computed that the work done on the cannon is approximately proportional to the caloric produced, a strong indicator that the theory of caloric is faulty. Most scientists ignored Thompson's findings, however. The caloric theory of heat dominated scientific thinking for several decades after Thompson's work, but it slowly lost ground as more and more counterexamples accumulated to show that the theory has no basis in reality.

Sadi Carnot

One person who did accept Black's theory of caloric was the French engineer Sadi Carnot (1796–1832). Carnot's father, the writer, politician, and military leader Lazare Carnot, was involved in the political turmoil that plagued France throughout Sadi's life. Lazare spent time in exile when the French Revolution turned sour and political executions became the norm. He returned to

France with the rise of Napoléon and served Napoléon both as minister of war and as minister of the interior. When Napoléon was finally defeated in 1815, Lazare again went into exile. In addition to participating in political and military activities, Lazare was a noted writer on mathematics and mechanics.

As his father was, Sadi Carnot was caught up in the chaos that gripped his native country. As a youth he benefited from the education he received from his father, who taught him mathematics and science. Later he attended the École Polytechnique, one of the leading scientific institutions of the day. Sadi Carnot did not have much opportunity to apply what he learned, however, because much of his brief adult life was spent in the military. Carnot's time in military service was marked by numerous disputes about assignments, promotions, and seniority. It was not until 1819, when he retired from active duty and went into reserve status, that he began to think about science.

Carnot's experience led him to believe that part of the reason Britain had defeated France under Napoléon was that Britain's technology, which was based on the steam engine, was much more advanced than French technology. He remarked that the steam engine had become as important to Britain's self-defense as its navy. Furthermore British technology, which was based on the work of a handful of self-taught engineers and inventors, especially James Watt, had surged ahead. This technological edge grated on Carnot, and he began to study and write about steam engines himself. His approach, however, was different from that of his contemporaries. Most engineers of the time concentrated on measurements and design details. Carnot began a search for general principles. He was especially interested in the relationship between heat and work. (In science *work* means exerting a force over a distance. A useful example of work is raising a weight, and in what follows we have several opportunities to interpret work as the raising of a weight.)

Carnot is remembered for a single slim book that he published, *Reflexions sur la puissance motrice du feu* (Reflections on the motive power of fire), which examines how heat can be used to produce motion: This is the meaning of the term *motive power.* In this

The Grand Coulee Dam. Waterpower provided a model for early scientists and engineers seeking to understand the workings of heat engines. (Library of Congress, Prints and Photographs Division, FSA/OWI Collection. Photo by H. Wayne Fuller)

highly original book Carnot developed a new way of looking at the world. By Carnot's time scientists had long been aware of the ways that forces affect motions. This is the content of Newton's three laws of motion, and Newton, Laplace, and others had worked to understand the implications of these laws. But nothing in this theory takes into account the role of heat. Carnot recognized that heat, too, is a motive force. Unequal heating of the atmosphere causes the winds. The source of rain and snow is water that is evaporated off the surface of the oceans. The water vapor then condenses and falls to the surface as precipitation. Heat is what causes the evaporation. Without heat there can be no weather. He also recognized that eruptions of volcanoes are, in the end, thermal (heat-driven) processes. Without heat life would be impossible. Carnot begins his book with a list of phenomena that are heat-driven. He demonstrates that the study of heat is a field unto itself.

Carnot accepted Black's ideas about caloric, a sort of heating fluid that always flows from warmer regions to cooler ones. To understand how Carnot incorporated these ideas into his own theory of heat engines, it is helpful to think about water turbines: Water always flows from higher elevations to lower ones. Engineers build dams to raise the water level on the upstream side of the dam. They then use pipes to direct the flowing water past turbines. The flowing water causes the turbines to spin, and the spinning motion of the turbines is then harnessed to do work. As the moving water pushes against the turbine, the water slows, but it does not stop. It flows past the turbine, down a pipe, and back into the river. No less water exits the pipe that directs it away from the turbine than enters the pipe that directs it toward the turbine. The water does its work, but the mass of the water is conserved.

The turbines that convert the motion of the water into work vary in their efficiency. For a given amount of water, moving at a given speed, some turbines "capture" more of the water's energy than others. To appreciate how we might measure the efficiency of a turbine, we can imagine installing a shunt on the downstream side of the turbine so that all the water that flows past the turbine is shunted into a pool. Now imagine using the turbine to drive a water pump. We can use the water pump to pump the water in the pool back upstream, where it can flow through the turbine again. If we could use this system to pump all of the water that flowed out of the turbine back upstream, we would have created a perpetual motion machine: (1) The water drives the turbine. (2) The turbine drives the pump. (3) The pump recirculates the water. Such a system could continue forever without any additional input from the outside. This does not happen—it cannot happen—in practice, but we can picture a turbine's efficiency as the degree to which it can approach this situation.

Carnot visualized caloric much as we have just described water. He saw a steam engine as working in much the same way as the water turbine we have just described. The high temperature of the boiler of a steam engine corresponds to the upstream side of the dam. The low temperature of the environment corresponds to the downstream side of the dam. Just as the water flows downstream, Carnot imagines the caloric flowing from the hotter thermal reservoir to the cooler thermal reservoir. (The expression *thermal reservoir*, or simply *reservoir*, has since become part of the standard vocabulary in the science of thermodynamics.) As the heat flows from the hot reservoir to the cold reservoir, the steam engine enables the user to convert some of the energy of the flowing caloric into useful work, but just as the water turbine does not convert all of the water's energy of motion into work, the steam engine does not convert all of the moving caloric into work. Some of the caloric flows right past the steam engine into the cooler reservoir. The question then is, How much work can be extracted from the caloric as it flows from the high temperature reservoir to the low?

To answer this question, Carnot imagined a special type of heat engine that is today called a Carnot engine. It is not possible actually to build a Carnot engine, although some engines that have been built in the lab function almost as a Carnot engine does. The fact, however, that a Carnot engine exists only in the imagination of engineers and scientists does not make it any less useful. The Carnot engine is an extremely important concept in understanding heat energy.

To appreciate the usefulness of a Carnot engine, some knowledge of its theoretical properties is helpful. A Carnot engine operates between a high-temperature reservoir and a low-temperature reservoir. It is generally described as a single cylinder that is closed off by a piston. Enclosed within the cylinder is a gas, the *working fluid*. Heat is transferred to and from the gas in the cylinder via a sequence of carefully controlled steps. At each step the piston is either raised or lowered. At the completion of the cycle the Carnot engine has produced some work—how much work depends on the temperature difference between the two reservoirs and the size of the engine— and the temperature and volume of the working fluid inside the cylinder have been precisely restored to what they had been before the cycle began. This restoration is an important characteristic of the engine: The Carnot engine is a cyclic engine. It repeats the same procedure with the same results over and over again.

Carnot mathematically demonstrated that his theoretical engine had a number of remarkable properties. First, Carnot's imaginary engine is remarkably efficient. The *efficiency* of a heat engine is defined as the ratio of the work done to the total amount of heat (caloric) absorbed. The larger the percentage of the absorbed heat that is converted into work, the more efficient the engine is. Carnot's engine is the most efficient of all (cyclic) heat engines. If it could be built it would be not only more efficient than any cyclic heat engine that has been built, but at least as efficient as any cyclic heat engine that can be built.

Second, Carnot discovered that the efficiency of the Carnot engine depended only on the difference in temperature between the high- and low-temperature reservoirs. In other words any Carnot engine operating between the same two reservoirs would have the same efficiency. It does not matter whether the working fluid in the engine is steam or some other gas. Any Carnot engine operating between the same two heat reservoirs performs as every other Carnot engine does. Because all Carnot engines operating between the same two heat reservoirs are equally efficient, and because even the best-made engines are still slightly less efficient than a Carnot engine, Carnot engines have become a sort of yardstick against which the efficiency of all designs of heat engines can be compared.

Carnot's insights into heat engines are remarkable because they reveal strict and permanent limitations on the efficiency of all heat engines. In retrospect Carnot's accomplishments are even more astonishing because he based his work on the caloric theory of Black. Today we know that Black's caloric theory of heat is seriously flawed, but Carnot's conclusions have stood the test of time.

Carnot's book was well received, but he did not publish anything further. This is not to say that he stopped thinking about heat engines. His later unpublished papers have been preserved, and from these papers it is clear that he continued to grapple with the problems involved. Soon after completing his masterpiece, Carnot made a disconcerting discovery: The caloric theory is wrong. Carnot had based his book on the caloric theory and later concluded that the caloric theory of heat was flawed. Instead Carnot began to perceive heat as "motive power"; that is, heat (caloric) can be converted to motive power and motive power converted to heat. The exchange is exact: The amount of heat lost *equals* the amount of motive power gained, and vice versa. This is a deep insight into nature, and Carnot took this to be an axiom, a law of nature. With these insights Carnot had essentially discovered what would later be known as the first law of thermodynamics, one of the most important of all natural laws.

Carnot's later ideas about the relationship between heat and work were not widely circulated. He made no immediate attempt

CALCULATING THE EFFICIENCY OF A CARNOT ENGINE

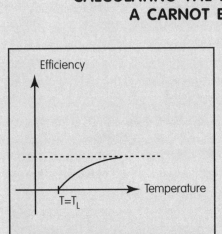

Graph demonstrating how the efficiency of a Carnot engine increases as the temperature difference between the upper and lower reservoirs increases. The temperature of the lower reservoir is usually taken to be that of the environment, a temperature over which engineers have little control. Consequently the independent variable is T_h, the operating temperature of the engine.

The Carnot engine is the most efficient heat engine that can operate between a given high-temperature reservoir and a given low-temperature reservoir. In other words once the temperature of both reservoirs is determined, no cyclic engine operating between these two reservoirs can convert a higher percentage of heat into work than the Carnot engine. The concept of efficiency is very important because heat generally costs money. Whether we obtain our heat from the burning of fossil fuels or the splitting of the atom—and these two sources are responsible for almost all of the heat generated at power plants—we must pay for every unit of heat produced. Unfortunately much of the heat is wasted in the sense that it cannot be converted into work. Instead, the "wasted" heat flows right through whatever heat engine is in use and out into the environment. Although some of that heat could be converted into work if a more efficient heat engine were employed, some of the waste is unpreventable. The Carnot engine tells us how much additional energy can be converted into work with a better designed and maintained engine and how much heat cannot be converted into work. So how efficient is a Carnot engine?

The algebraic formula relating efficiency to the temperatures of the reservoirs is simple. Let the letter E represent the efficiency of the engine. An efficiency rating of 100 percent means that all of the heat is converted into work. (An efficiency rating of 100 percent is not possible.) An efficiency rating of 0 percent means that none of the heat is converted into work. To make use of this formula the temperatures of the two thermal reservoirs must be measured in degrees Kelvin, a temperature scale that is commonly used in the sciences. (The temperature 273.16K [Kelvin]) corresponds to 0°C and an increase of 1°C corresponds to an increase of 1K.) The letters T_H and T_L represent, respectively, the temperatures of the high- and low-temperature reservoirs measured in degrees Kelvin. The formula for the efficiency of the Carnot engine is $E = (1 - T_L/T_H) \times 100$. Notice that the greater the difference between T_H and T_L, the smaller the fraction T_L/T_H becomes. The smaller T_L/T_H is, the higher the efficiency of the Carnot engine. Notice, too, that since T_L/T_H is never 0, the engine cannot operate at 100 percent efficiency.

This formula also shows that engines that operate between two temperature reservoirs that are at almost the same temperature are not at all efficient. For example, heat engines have been designed to produce electrical power by operating between the warm, upper layers of tropical ocean water and the cool waters that flow along the ocean floor. This is called Ocean Thermal Energy Conversion (OTEC) technology. There have been demonstration plants tested in Hawaii in 1979, a different design was tested in Hawaii from 1993 until 1998, and a third OTEC plant was tested on the island-state of Nauru in 1982. The upper ocean temperature in these areas hovers around 300K (80°F or 27°C) and the temperature of the water near the ocean floor measures about 277K (39°F or 4°C). A Carnot engine operating between these two reservoirs would be 8 percent efficient; that is, if it absorbed 100 units of heat from the upper layer of ocean, it could convert 8 percent of that heat to work, and no heat engine can do better. Full-scale, practical plants, however, would probably operate at an efficiency of about 4 percent. In order to obtain useful amounts of work from engines with such low efficiencies, they have to be operated on an enormous scale.

The simple efficiency equation for a Carnot engine also explains the attraction of heat engines that operate at very high temperatures. Engineers are generally unable to do anything about the temperature of the lower heat reservoir. The lower heat reservoir is generally the environment, and nothing can be done about the temperature of the environment. To obtain a more efficient engine—one that wastes less heat and produces more work from the same amount of thermal energy—the only alternative is to raise the temperature of the higher-temperature reservoir.

to publish them. Perhaps he delayed so that he could ponder how his rejection of the caloric theory affected the conclusions of his already-published book. Whatever the reason, he delayed too long. Carnot died at the young age of 36, a victim of cholera.

James Prescott Joule

Experiments that indicated that caloric is not a conserved property continued to accumulate, but no set of experiments was definitive until the work of the British physicist James Prescott Joule (1818–89). Joule was independently wealthy. He did not need to study anything, but he decided to devote his life to science. He studied electricity, heat, and the relationship between heat and work. One of his first discoveries was that a current flowing in a wire produces heat. Most of his contemporaries still subscribed to the caloric theory and, consequently, believed that heat (caloric) cannot be produced because it is conserved—that is (according to the caloric theory), an increase in heat in one location must be accompanied by a decrease of heat in another location. In Joule's case this meant that an increase in temperature in one part of his circuit should be accompanied by a decrease in temperature somewhere else. Joule showed that this is not the case.

Joule performed a series of experiments to try to identify the relationship between heat and work. In an early experiment he placed an electrical resistor in a bath of water. (Today we might say that a resistor is a device that

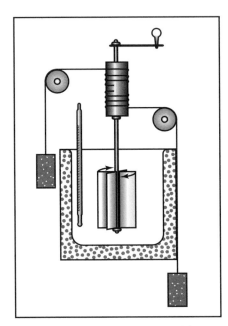

Diagram of an apparatus used by Joule to investigate the relationship between work and heat

converts electrical energy into heat energy.) He placed wires at each end of the resistor and connected these wires to a small generator. The generator was connected to weights. As the weights descended under the force of gravity, the generator turned and caused electricity to flow through the resistor. Heat, or what was then called caloric, was created at the resistor. The heat flowed out of the resistor and into the cooler water. The temperature of the water increased, and this increase in temperature was measured by a thermometer that had been immersed in the water.

How did this allow Joule to compare work and heat? Weight is force. Joule knew how heavy his weights were. The distance the weights descended was easy to measure. *Work* is defined as force times distance. So Joule could compute how much work had been done on the system. The increase in temperature of the water was likewise easy to measure; the change in the water's temperature enabled Joule to compute how much heat had flowed into the water from the resistor. It was a simple equation: On one side of the equation was the work performed; on the other side was the heat that had been added to the water. Joule had found a relationship between work and heat.

The main problem with which Joule was concerned was the identification of the "mechanical equivalent of heat." Essentially he wanted to know how much heat has to be expended to produce one unit of work, and vice versa. In Joule's view caloric (heat) is not a conserved quantity. Instead heat is one form of energy, and different forms of energy can be converted one to another. Each form of energy can be converted into work, and the process can be reversed: Work can be converted into heat as well. But this kind of thinking is not precise enough to form a legitimate theory. If work and heat can be converted one into another, then it should be possible to determine how many units of work equal one unit of heat and how many units of heat equal one unit of work.

His first goal was to prove that work and heat are, in a sense, two sides of the same coin. He continued to devise and perform carefully crafted and executed experiments. Each experiment approached the same problem—the identification of the mechanical equivalent of heat—from a somewhat different perspective.

Perhaps his best-known experiment involved placing a paddle into a container of water. The paddle was driven by falling weights. As the weights descended, the paddle spun around in the water. In this experiment just as in the one described previously, gravity does the work by pulling the weights down. This work is transmitted to the water by the spinning paddle. The result is measured by a thermometer. The increase in temperature of the water enabled Joule to compute how much heat has gone into the water. What Joule discovered was that as the paddle spun in the water, the temperature of the water increased slightly. Joule was essentially creating "caloric" by stirring water. The heat was the result of friction between the paddle and the water, between the water and the walls of the container, and inside the water itself as one region of water flowed past another. The resulting friction raised the temperature of the entire system. Joule had created heat, and he had done so in a way that enabled him to state how much work had been performed in the creation of the heat.

Joule's experiments disproved the caloric theory. By performing variants of the same experiment he was able to show in a rough way that the amount of heat produced for a given amount of work is independent of the way the work is performed. It was a fairly convincing set of experiments, although from a practical point of view, there was still substantial doubt about the exact value of the mechanical equivalent of heat. The reason is that Joule's experiments are difficult to run. Small amounts of heat escape through the walls of the container, and there are frictional losses in the experimental apparatus itself. Consequently the results Joule obtained from his various experiments were only roughly similar. His experiments led many scientists to question the caloric theory of heat, but there was still much uncertainty about what the truth was.

The First Law of Thermodynamics

The work of Joule and Carnot was the foundation on which the science of thermodynamics was built. The first person to recognize how Joule's and Carnot's ideas about work and heat could be incorporated into a coherent theory was the German physicist and mathematician Rudolf Clausius (1822–88). Clausius was the first to state what is now known as the first law of thermodynamics.

As a child Rudolf Clausius attended a small school at which his father was principal. As he became older he was drawn equally to history and mathematics. He eventually chose to study mathematics and physics. His approach to physics was always a very mathematical one. He was a student at the University of Berlin and Halle University, where he received a Ph.D. His dissertation was about the

Rudolph Clausius was the first to understand the principles on which the science of thermodynamics is based. (Science Museum, London/Topham-HIP/The Image Works)

color of the sky: He sought a scientific explanation for why the sky is blue during the day and red and orange around sunrise and sunset. Clausius described the phenomenon in terms of the reflection and refraction of sunlight. His explanation was not quite correct: The sky's colors are actually caused by the scattering of light. The correct explanation for the sky's color was later proposed by the British mathematician and physicist William Thomson (1824–1907), also known as Lord Kelvin, who along with Clausius developed the fundamental ideas that lie at the heart of the science of heat, work, and energy.

Clausius was not one for ease. He worked for the advancement of science throughout his life, occasionally moving from one university to another in search of the best place to do his research. But scientific research was not his only passion. As well as a mathematician and scientist, Clausius was a staunch German nationalist. When the Franco-Prussian War began in 1870, Clausius was already well into middle age. He was too old for the rigors of fighting, but he volunteered to serve in the ambulance corps along with some of his students. While helping to carry the wounded off the field during battle, he was severely wounded in the leg. The wound bothered him for the remainder of his life. At the conclusion of his military service in 1871, Clausius returned to academia, where he was as determined to complete his academic service as he had been to complete his war service. It is said that even toward the end of his life—even from his deathbed—he was still engaged in his work as a teacher.

When Clausius was a student, the field of thermodynamics was still dominated by the ideas of Joseph Black. In the mid-1700s Black had classified heat by its effects on matter rather than on a deeper analysis of its nature. This type of analysis probably advanced understanding when Black proposed it, but by the 1840s it had become a hindrance.

Part of the difficulty that Clausius faced in identifying what we now call the first law of thermodynamics was understanding the role of latent heat. When a heat engine completes a cycle, three quantities can be measured: (1) the work performed by the engine, (2) the amount of heat transferred from the higher-temperature reservoir to the engine, and (3) the amount of heat transferred from the engine to the lower-temperature reservoir. When the engine is running, some heat is always transferred to the lower-temperature reservoir. The problem is that the amount of heat transferred to the lower-temperature reservoir seems smaller than the amount of heat that has been drawn from the high-temperature reservoir. Clausius's contemporaries debated about what had happened to the "missing" heat. Had the missing heat been converted into work, as Joule had asserted, or had it become latent and so not detectable as a change in temperature? Some scientists of the time, reluctant to abandon the idea of conservation of caloric, used the idea of latent heat to prop up the old caloric model.

Clausius, however, rejected the theory of conservation of heat. Missing heat had been detected in the operation of every heat engine, but there was no reason to suppose that it had "gone latent." Clausius found ample proof in Joule's experiments that the missing heat had been converted into work. Incorporating the ideas of his predecessors into a single unified concept, Clausius asserts that it is not heat that is being conserved in a given system but rather energy. According to Clausius heat does not just flow through engines in the way water flows through turbines; heat is *converted* by engines during the process of doing work. In a closed system (a system cut off from its surroundings) the energy of the system cannot change. If the system does interact with its surroundings, then the energy of the system fluctuates as heat is transmitted across the boundary and work is done.

Work and heat are related through the energy of the system. In the absence of work the energy of a system—for the moment, imagine the system as a cylinder of gas sealed with a piston—can be changed only by the transmission of heat across the system boundary. This was the type of phenomenon that had originally caught the attention of early scientists. This is also why recognizing their mistake was difficult for them: In the absence of work no heat is converted, so the caloric theory appears valid. Alternatively the energy of the system can be changed by work. If the system performs work on its environment—for example, the system may raise a weight—then the energy of the system decreases by an amount equal to the amount of work performed. This conversion into work had been incorrectly interpreted as heat's becoming latent. Furthermore both processes—the transmission of heat and the production of work—can occur simultaneously. In this case the change in energy of the system is equal to the sum of the work done and the heat transmitted. Clausius asserted that the change in energy of a system can be *completely* accounted for by the sum of the heat flow into or out of the system and the work performed. This result, called the first law of thermodynamics, is often stated like this:

(Change in energy of a system) =
– (work done by the system) + (heat flow across the boundary)

(The negative sign preceding the work term indicates that when the system performs work, the energy decreases. If heat flows out of the system, we give it a minus sign; if heat flows into the system, the sign is reversed.) Here is how Clausius expressed the first law:

> The energy of the universe is constant.

Clausius's statement of the first law of thermodynamics strikes many people as more philosophical than mathematical. Our statement of the first law in terms of "the change in energy of the system" is meant to convey more of the mathematical flavor involved. Often the first law of thermodynamics is described in the language of cylinders and pistons. Clausius's description, however, does the most justice to the importance of the first law, because it conveys some sense of the scope of the discovery. The discovery of energy and its relationship to heat and work is one of the great milestones in the history of science. It is a cornerstone of modern scientific thought.

The first law is more than an important principle. The statement that the rate of change of energy equals the rate of heating and working of the system allows the mathematically inclined scientist to express his or her ideas in terms of very specific mathematical equations. Like the conservation of momentum and conservation of mass, the first law of thermodynamics can be written in terms of a differential equation. Scientists can tailor these types of equations to the particular situations in which they are interested. A solution to this type of differential equation is a function that represents the energy of the system.

Clausius established a firm link between mathematics and science, but was he right? How do we know that the first law of thermodynamics is valid everywhere and in all situations? This is, after all, what Clausius was hoping to convey with his extremely broad statement about energy and the universe. The answer to the question about the universal validity of the first law is surprisingly simple (and to some people not altogether satisfying): We "know" that the first law is true because no one has ever observed a situation in which the first law is false. No one, for example, has ever seen energy consumed or created. Of course only a few hundred years ago many scientists spent their working life studying physics without ever observing the consumption or the creation of heat (caloric), whereas today these kinds of observations pose no problem at all to the curious high school student. Will we one day be able to point to exceptions to the first law of thermodynamics? The best that can be said about the validity of the first law is that since it was first formulated by Clausius, no scientist has ever erred in assuming its validity.

Despite the importance of his discovery and despite his recognition of its importance to science, Clausius also recognized that the first law is, in a sense, deficient. The first law is true, he knew, but it is not true enough. In his study of heat Clausius had realized that there is another law of nature, now known as the second law of thermodynamics, that further constrains the types of processes that can occur.

The Second Law of Thermodynamics

The second law of thermodynamics is the result of the work of Rudolf Clausius and William Thomson, also known as Lord Kelvin. Clausius was the first to state it. He noticed that the first law was, in a sense, incomplete, because it does not make a strong enough distinction between *possible* processes and *impossible* ones. Clausius is right: Every system changes in such a way that the first law of thermodynamics remains valid. The problem is that there are many processes that never occur that nevertheless *would* conform to the first law of thermodynamics if they did occur.

To illustrate the problem, imagine using a block of ice as a heater. We usually imagine ice as being without heat, but this is never the case. Although a great deal of heat must be removed from a large body of water to freeze it into a solid block of ice, there is still a great deal of heat left in the body even after it has frozen solid. This statement is easily proved. If we place a container of liquid nitrogen on a block of ice, the liquid nitrogen boils. (The boiling point of nitrogen at atmospheric pressure is about –321°F (–196°C).) The heat that boils the nitrogen is the heat that has flowed out of the ice. As the nitrogen boils, the block of ice gets even colder, indicating that there has been heat in the

The Corliss steam engine of 1876. Engineers discovered that no matter how they designed their heat engines, not all of the heat produced could be converted into work. (Science Museum, London/Topham-HIP/ The Image Works)

block all along. If we can easily boil liquid nitrogen by placing it on a block of (water) ice, why cannot we also boil liquid water in the same way? It is easy enough to imagine how this might occur: We place a container of water on a block of ice. The heat from the block of ice flows into the container of water, causing the liquid water to begin to boil. Of course this never happens, but could it happen? There is nothing in the first law of thermodynamics to rule out this possibility.

Clausius thought about Carnot's engine in a slightly more technical vein. Carnot imagined his engine forming a conduit for heat as the heat flows from the higher-temperature thermal reservoir to the lower-temperature one. Heat, Carnot imagined, flows from hot to cold in just the same way that water flows from higher elevations to lower ones. This analogy between the flow of heat and the flow of water is at the heart of the caloric theory, but Clausius had rejected the caloric theory. Unfortunately there is nothing in his new theory to substitute for the idea that heat, as water does, always seeks its own level. So theoretically the possibility exists that an engine, placed between a higher-temperature and a lower-temperature thermal reservoir, can run on heat that flows from the lower-temperature reservoir "up" to the higher-temperature reservoir. Of course, no one has ever seen this occur, but there is nothing in the first law to rule it out, either. In the case of the heat engine's running on "backward"-flowing heat, the first

Multi-Grain Waffles with Strawberries

1. Combine the strawberries with the granulated sugar and let them sit for about a half hour until they release some juice. Preheat your waffle iron. (Optional: Coat with cooking spray.) Mix the buttermilk with the oats and let stand for about 15 minutes.

2. Whisk the flours, wheat germ or cornmeal, baking powder, baking soda, salt, and cinnamon in a large bowl. Stir the eggs, brown sugar, oil, and vanilla into the buttermilk/oat mixture. Add the wet mixture to the dry mixture, and mix just until everything is moistened.

3. Use approximately 2/3 cup batter to cover an 8-by-8-inch waffle iron. (Tip for larger waffle irons: Use 1/3 cup per square.) Cook each waffle until the steaming slows down a lot—approximately 4–5 minutes for golden brown, crunchy waffles. Keep warm in the oven while you cook the rest.

Learn more about our can-do Medicare plan—Kaiser Permanente Senior Advantage (HMO).
Call today for a FREE* Medicare Decision Guide.
Toll free **1-877-653-4210** (TTY 1-888-758-6054), seven days a week, 8 a.m. to 8 p.m.

Find more healthy recipes at **kp.org/senioradvantage/ga/cando**.

H1170_N002322 (10/2009)

Multi-Grain Waffles with Strawberries

Ingredients

Serves 8

4 cups	strawberries, hulled and sliced
3 Tbsp.	granulated sugar
2 cups	nonfat buttermilk
1/2 cup	rolled oats
2/3 cup	whole wheat flour
2/3 cup	all-purpose flour
	Optional: Substitute 1 1/3 cups of white whole wheat flour for the two flours.
1/4 tsp.	wheat germ or cornmeal
1 1/2 tsp.	baking powder
1 tsp.	ground cinnamon
1/2 tsp.	baking soda
1/4 tsp.	salt
2	large eggs, lightly beaten
1/4 cup	packed brown sugar
1 Tbsp.	canola oil
2 tsp.	vanilla extract

Nutrition Information per Serving

Calories: 213
Fat: 4 gm
Saturated Fat: 1 gm

Trans Fat: 0 gm
Cholesterol: 55 mg
Carbohydrate: 36 gm

Fiber: 4 gm
Sodium: 329 mg
Protein: 8 gm

law is satisfied provided that the decrease in energy of the lower-temperature reservoir equals the sum of the work performed by the engine plus the amount of heat rejected to the higher-temperature reservoir. The theory of heat is still incomplete.

To complete his theory Clausius asserted the existence of a second law of thermodynamics. The second law was to become a major theme of Clausius's life. He wrote a number of papers about it, carefully stating and restating it, weighing one interpretation of the second law against another. Part of the reason that he spent so much time writing about the second law is that he was asserting something that is quite new in the history of science. The second law is fundamentally different from previous natural laws. It is negative. It states the impossibility of certain processes. By contrast the conservation laws are all positive. They state that some property is conserved. The mathematical form of the second law is also different from the form of all previous laws of nature. Unlike conservation laws, which are written as equalities, the mathematical statement of the second law of thermodynamics is an *inequality*. The scientific, mathematical, and philosophical implications of the second law continue to draw the attention of thoughtful people to this day.

Clausius's first attempt to grapple with this newfound physical principle rested on the observation that when two objects of different temperatures are placed in contact with each other, heat always flows from the warmer body to the cooler one. The warmer body always cools, and the cooler body always warms. The reverse never happens. It is never the case that when two bodies at different temperatures are placed in contact with each other, heat flows from the cooler body into the warmer body. If this impossible transformation could happen, then the warm body would become warmer and the cool body would become cooler still. Those observations seem almost too obvious to bother mentioning, but Clausius carried them a step further. He claimed that it is not possible to devise a cyclic machine or system of cyclic machines whose only effect is to transfer heat from a low-temperature reservoir to a high-temperature reservoir. (A refrigerator, of course, transfers heat from the freezer to the warmer air in the kitchen, but in doing so it also produces a lot of additional heat of its own. The refrigerator does not violate the second law of thermodynamics.) The second law of thermodynamics has been phrased and rephrased a great deal since Clausius's time. Here is one version of what is usually called Clausius's statement of the second law of thermodynamics:

> It is impossible to construct a cyclic engine whose only effect is the transfer of heat from a body at a lower temperature to one at a higher temperature.

It is, admittedly, a very peculiar natural law. First, it is, as we have already pointed out, a negative statement. Negative statements cannot be proved experimentally: There is no experiment that can rule out the existence of another experiment that does not conform to the second law. Nevertheless, no experiment that violates the second law has ever been devised. In fact as we soon see, any experiment that did violate the second law would have very peculiar implications for the universe. Second, though the second law is held up as a universal law of nature, it is often stated in terms of the impossibility of designing a certain type of refrigerator. (It is, after all, the function of a refrigerator to transfer heat from a body at low temperature, such as frozen foods, to one at higher temperature, the air in the kitchen.) There is nothing else in science to compare with the second law of thermodynamics.

In addition to ruling out the possibility of certain types of physical transformations of heat and work, the second law of thermodynamics has profound philosophical implications. A good example of this type of implication is the concept of *heat death*. An exposition of the idea can be found in the work of the other founder of thermodynamics, William Thomson (Lord Kelvin).

William Thomson was born in Belfast, Ireland. His mother died when he was six. His father, a mathematician, taught William and his older brother, James. Their father must have been a good teacher, because James enrolled in the University of Glasgow at age 11 and William enrolled at age 10. William Thomson published his first mathematics papers when he was still a teenager. He wrote about a mathematical method for describing the flow of heat through solids, a method that had been recently pioneered by the French mathematician Jean-Baptiste-Joseph Fourier (1768–1830). Later Thomson enrolled in Cambridge University, and it was from Cambridge that he graduated.

During his years at Glasgow and Cambridge Thomson had proved himself an able mathematician, but he wanted to learn more about the experimental side of science. After graduation he moved to Paris, where he worked with the French physicist and chemist Henri-Victor Regnault (1810–78). Regnault was a tireless experimentalist. He tested and measured the physical properties of various gases and liquids. Thomson's stay at Regnault's laboratory resulted in a paper, published in 1849, "Account of Carnot's Theory of the Motive Power of Heat; with Numerical Results derived from Regnault's Experiments on Steam." Thomson eventually joined the faculty at the University of Glasgow, where he remained the rest of his working life.

Scientists today best remember Thomson—or Kelvin—for his contributions to the theory of thermodynamics and his work in electricity and magnetism. (The temperature scale most commonly used in science, the Kelvin scale, is named after him.) During his own life, however, Kelvin was at least as famous for his work on telegraph cables. By the middle of the 19th century, many European cities were linked by the telegraph. The telegraph had also become an important part of life in North America as well. People began to consider the possibility of linking North America to Europe via a 3,000-mile (4,800-km) undersea cable. Kelvin understood the physics of sending an electrical signal through a long cable. He was hired as a consultant on the project, but his ideas were not incorporated into the first attempt to lay the cable. The attempt failed and Kelvin's ideas were used during later successful attempts. His contributions made Britain a world leader in electronic communications.

Kelvin was a more conservative scientist than Clausius. He had recognized for some time that there were problems in the theory of heat, but knowing that something is wrong is not the same as knowing what is right. Kelvin recognized that Joule's experiments indicated that heat is not conserved, and he knew that the development of the science of thermodynamics depended on the identification of a conserved property, but at the time he could think of no alternative to the conservation of caloric. Kelvin did not entirely abandon the theory of the conservation of caloric until he read Clausius's paper.

Kelvin formulated his own version of the second law of thermodynamics, and today both versions are taught side by side. Although they look different, one can prove that Clausius's version is true if and only if Kelvin's version of the second law is true, so they are completely equivalent. What makes Kelvin's version worth considering is that he began from a different point of view. In his article "Account of Carnot's Theory of the Motive Power of Heat," Kelvin imagined two bodies, a warm one and a cool one, and a heat engine placed between the two bodies. The engine can harness the flow of heat to do work. Alternatively he supposed that the two bodies are simply placed in contact with each other with no engine between them. Heat then flows directly from the warm body to the cool one. In the absence of phase changes the warm body cools and the temperature of the cool body increases. But what, Kelvin asked, happens to the work that could have been produced by the heat engine?

Kelvin's answer is that the work is lost. It cannot be recovered. When heat *dissipates*—when it flows between two thermal reservoirs and evens out their temperatures—the work that could have been produced by those two reservoirs is lost forever. What Kelvin recognized is that heat dissipation is inevitable. It often occurs slowly, but it goes on continuously. In his book Carnot emphasized the motive

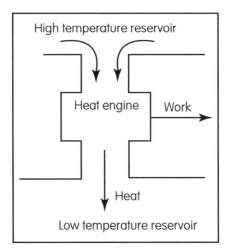

When the engine is not present, the work that might have been accomplished by the heat that flowed from the higher- to the lower-temperature reservoir is irrevocably lost.

ENTROPY

Clausius's first paper on thermodynamics was just the beginning. He was interested in formulating a mathematical statement of the second law, and to this end he defined the concept of entropy. Entropy is a mathematical function with a physical interpretation. It conveys information about the amount of energy that can be transferred between thermodynamic systems in the form of work. It is through the concept of entropy that Clausius was able to express his ideas about thermodynamics in mathematical language.

For a particular system the value of the entropy function can range from 0 to a maximal value. The value of the entropy for a particular system at any point in time depends on the physical characteristics of that system—temperature, for example, is an important factor. The smaller the value of the entropy, the more of the system's energy can be converted to work. A large value for the entropy means that very little of the system's energy can be transformed into work.

What is often of interest to scientists, however, is not so much the entropy of the system as the change of entropy. Imagine a system consisting of a cyclic heat engine operating between a high-temperature thermal reservoir and a low-temperature thermal reservoir. Practically speaking, no system can be completely isolated from its surroundings, so we can expect some heat to flow between our system and the environment. Suppose that we compute the change of entropy of the environment caused by this transfer of heat. We can, of course, also compute the change of entropy that resulted from the operation of our not-quite-isolated system. Finally, we add the two entropy changes to get the change in the total entropy. When we do this we get a very famous inequality, which we can write like this:

(Change in total entropy) = (change in entropy of environment) + (change in system entropy) ≥ 0

This inequality, however, actually applies to *all* processes. In other words no matter what we do, no matter what processes we consider, the *total* entropy never decreases. Because entropy is a measure of the energy that can be converted into work—the greater the entropy, the less energy we can convert to work—this statement is a mathematical version of Kelvin's ruminations about lost work. In most natural processes the change in the total entropy is positive. As a consequence the longer the universe "runs on," the less energy is available to do work. Clausius also formulated his version of the second law so that it does not depend on the concept of a refrigerator. Here is a commonly quoted version of his more philosophical statement of the second law:

The entropy of the universe tends toward its maximal value.

power of heat. Heat drives all the processes on which life depends, but heat flows only when there are temperature differences. These temperature differences are slowly, continually, and inexorably disappearing. As the temperature differences disappear, so does the motive power of heat. Everything that depends on the transmission of heat begins to slow and eventually everything stops. This occurs not because energy disappears; energy cannot disappear. It is conserved. Instead energy becomes unavailable to do work. This peculiar state of affairs, in which all thermal processes cease, is *heat death*. It is the final state of the universe. The subject of heat death has inspired many interesting philosophical papers.

Kelvin's ruminations on the loss of the availability of energy are reflected in what is usually called Kelvin's version of the second law:

> It is impossible to construct a cyclic machine whose only effect is to perform work using heat extracted from a single reservoir that is the same temperature throughout.

Like Clausius's version of the second law, Kelvin's version is a negative statement. It, too, states a basic law of nature in terms of the impossibility of constructing a certain type of machine. Kelvin used a heat engine in his formulation; Clausius used a refrigerator.

Notice that if Kelvin's formulation of the second law were false, then we could attach a cyclic heat engine to a single thermal reservoir—the surface of the Earth, for example—and run it as long as we wanted. The engine would have no other effect than that of cooling Earth's surface as it converted heat into work. Given the amount of thermal energy in the Earth, this would be, for all practical purposes, a perpetual motion machine. This kind of machine has never been constructed. The failure to build this type of device is one of the principal arguments supporting the truth of the second law of thermodynamics.

Energy is one of the most important concepts in science, and its importance has only increased in the years since Clausius published his discoveries. It is now a fundamental concept in understanding the inner workings of galaxies and the inner

Typical higher and lower temperatures and efficiencies for steam electric power plants

	TEMPERATURE, °C		EFFICIENCY, %	
	High	Low	Carnot	Actual
Large fossil-fuel plant	380	40	52	40
Boiling-water reactor	285	40	44	34
Pressurized-water reactor	315	40	47	34

workings of atoms. It is as important in the philosophy of science as it is in the design of refrigerators. It is, perhaps, the only physical principle to find such wide applicability. The discoveries of Clausius and Kelvin are among the most important in the history of science.

8

MODERN IDEAS ABOUT CONSERVATION LAWS

Ancient science was, for the most part, applied geometry. Mesopotamian and Greek insights into nature were almost exclusively geometric. The Mesopotamians sought to characterize the motions of the planets and the Sun across the sky without apparent concern for the underlying causes. The Greeks sought to determine the ratio of the distances between Earth and the Moon and Earth and the Sun. They sought to compute the circumference of Earth. They described the motions of the planets as the motions of spheres within spheres. Even Archimedes's description of the lever was essentially geometric in approach, depending as it did on the idea of symmetry.

Beginning in the Renaissance the ancient geometric understanding of nature was displaced by what appeared to be more fundamental insights. Geometry was not entirely abandoned, of course. Geometric reasoning has always been important in the physical sciences, but as scientists developed new ways of understanding nature, the importance of geometry to science diminished. New mathematics developed in conjunction with the new sciences. Some of the new mathematics was geometric, but some was not. Combined with the new scientific concepts, the new math greatly facilitated the search for a description of nature that is predictive. Scientists learned how to predict the position of previously undiscovered planets. They learned to predict the motion of projectiles and the amount of work that could be produced by a particular design of engine—even before the engine was constructed.

These were great successes, and they were followed by still other successes.

Central to scientific progress was the concept of the conservation law. Conservation laws became so important to science and mathematics that mathematicians began to develop a mathematical theory of conservation laws. The study of conservation laws led them back to geometry. This modern understanding of conservation laws is the result of the work of the German mathematician Emmy Noether (1882–1935).

Emmy Noether grew up in Erlangen, Germany, home to the University of Erlangen, an institution that boasted a number of distinguished mathematicians. Her father was a capable mathematician and was himself a member of the mathematics faculty at Erlangen. Emmy, however, did not immediately gravitate to mathematics. She showed facility with languages, and her original plan was to teach foreign languages in secondary schools. She even received her certification in English and French, but she never taught languages. Instead she turned her attention to mathematics. First, she studied mathematics at Erlangen. She also studied at Göttingen University and eventually earned a Ph.D. in mathematics at Erlangen.

Pursuing an advanced education in the mathematical sciences was a difficult career path for a woman in Germany at the time. Women were, with permission of the instructor, allowed to take individual courses. As a general rule, however, women were barred from completing the examinations necessary to become a full member of the faculty of a university. At Erlangen Noether sometimes

Emmy Noether, founder of the modern theory of conservation laws (Courtesy of the Bryn Mawr College Library)

taught a class for her father, but she did so without pay. Her mathematical talents, however, were eventually recognized by two of the most distinguished of all German mathematicians, David Hilbert and Felix Klein, both of whom were then at Göttingen. Noether moved to Göttingen 1915.

Initially Noether taught courses under Hilbert's name. Though both Klein and Hilbert advocated that the university offer her a position on the faculty, this request was denied. Other faculty members objected to the hiring of women. It took time to overcome some of the discrimination that she faced, and during this time she taught classes without pay. As word of her discoveries spread, however, mathematicians from outside Göttingen began to show up in her classes. In 1919 she was offered a position on the faculty.

Noether was Jewish, and in 1933, when the Nazis gained power in Germany, she, like other Jewish faculty members, lost her job. By this time, however, her contributions to mathematics had made her known to mathematicians throughout the world. Within a few months of her dismissal she left Germany for the United States. The remainder of her working life was spent at Bryn Mawr College, Bryn Mawr, Pennsylvania, and the Princeton Institute for Advanced Study, Princeton, New Jersey. Noether died within a few years of moving to the United States of complications that followed surgery.

Noether's main interest was algebra. Abstract algebra is the study of mathematical structure, and she had a particularly insightful approach to the subject. She is often described as one of the most creative algebraicists of the 20th century. By contrast her work in the study of conservation laws was just a brief interlude. She might not have become interested in the topic at all had not her chief sponsor at Göttingen, David Hilbert, asked her for help.

During Noether's stay at Göttingen several of the most prominent mathematicians at the university—and at the time Göttingen was home to some of the best mathematicians in the world—were hard at work studying the mathematical basis of Albert Einstein's newly published general theory of relativity. Ideas were changing quickly, and the mathematicians at Göttingen were in the thick of it. David Hilbert, for example, had published equations similar to those of Einstein within a few months of the date of Einstein's own papers.

Mathematically the problem with the equations that describe relativity theory is that they are very complex. Initially the goal was simply to try to understand what the equations imply about the physical structure of the universe. There were questions, for example, about the relationships between Einstein's theory and the theories of classical physics. In particular a number of mathematicians had questions about the role of conservation of energy in Einstein's model. Hilbert asked Noether for her help on this issue, and Noether, though her interests were in pure mathematics and not physics, agreed to examine the issue. She quickly identified a profound connection between conservation laws and geometry. Her ideas on this matter have had a permanent influence on mathematicians' and physicists' understanding of what a conservation law is.

Noether's discovery is that each conservation law is a statement about symmetry. In geometry symmetry is an important organizing principle. A visual image is symmetric about a line, for example, if we can draw a line through the image so that what lies on one side of the line is the mirror image of what lies on the other side of the line. This is an idea with which most of us are familiar. A frontal image of the human body, for example, is symmetric about the line that passes vertically through the center of the face. Mathematicians have generalized this idea in a number of ways. In mathematics there is symmetry with respect to a point, a line, and a plane, as well as other types of mathematical symmetry.

Noether discovered that each conservation law corresponds to a particular type of symmetry. In other words given a conservation law we can find a symmetry associated with it. Alternatively every symmetry of a certain type corresponds to a conservation law. This means that if we begin from the point of view of geometry—if we choose a particular symmetry from a set of symmetries—then it is, in theory, possible to determine a conservation law corresponding to this symmetry. Geometry and conservation laws turn out to be two sides of the same coin, and geometry was once again at the forefront of humanity's attempts to understand nature.

The details of Noether's discovery require quite a bit of mathematics, but if we apply her ideas to the conservation of energy we can get a feeling for the insight behind her discovery. To do this it is helpful to think of time as a kind of line. We can imagine moving (translating) ourselves either forward or backward along the line. In order for the law of conservation of energy to be valid there must exist a *translational symmetry* with respect to time. This means that regardless of how we might imagine moving back and forth through time, the amount of energy in an isolated system must remain constant.

To see why this must be so, imagine a heat engine operating between two bodies of different temperatures. As we run the heat engine, the temperatures of the two bodies become more and more alike. The closer the two temperatures become one to another, the less work our engine produces per unit of heat. In theory it is always possible to run our engine backward and use it as a heat pump so that it restores the two thermal reservoirs to their original state. If time is translationally symmetric (or what is the same thing: if the first law of thermodynamics is true), then the best we can expect from this procedure is to "break even." The work we performed on our engine in restoring the thermal reservoirs equals the work obtained by running our engine in the first place. Or, to put it more succinctly: "work in" equals "work out." But if, instead, translational symmetry fails, we can do better than this—better in the sense that we can run an engine at a "profit." In this case we simply choose a time to restore the thermal reservoirs when restoring the reservoirs requires less work than we have already obtained in work from the engine. If this were possible then at the end of the cycle our machine would have produced more work than it consumed in heat. Such machines are impossible to build: They violate the first law of thermodynamics. Translational symmetry with respect to time is valid only if energy is conserved, and energy is conserved only if translational symmetry holds with respect to time. Noether showed that the geometric property of symmetry is a central organizing principle of nature.

Olga Oleinik

Roughly a century after Clausius first proposed the second law of thermodynamics, scientists and engineers were still wondering what to do with it. To be sure the second law is an important insight into how nature works. The second law enables scientists to compute the maximal efficiency of a heat engine or declare the ultimate fate of the universe (heat death). It is less useful, however, for predicting the actual efficiency of an engine, and some scientists complained that it revealed little about what would happen between now and the final thermal collapse of the universe. The second law of thermodynamics is a negative assertion, and knowing what cannot happen is just not as useful as calculating what must happen.

A principal difference between the mathematical expression of the second law and the mathematical expression of the conservation laws described earlier is that whereas conservation laws are equalities, the second law of thermodynamics is an inequality. Mathematically this means that conservation laws can be written as differential *equations.* They relate the rate of change of a property, such as momentum, mass, or energy, to one or more measurable quantities, such as force, mass flow across the boundary, or work and heat flow. For a scientist differential equations are useful

Olga Oleinik successfully applied new mathematics and an abstraction of the idea of entropy to the mathematical study of discontinuous processes such as shock waves. (Courtesy of Gregory A. Chechkin)

because they serve as a bridge between what the scientist can measure and what the scientist can, in principle, calculate. A differential equation is a method of identifying one particular function among many: If the differential equation is properly posed, then it can have only one solution, the function of interest. When the second law is expressed mathematically, however, we get a differential *inequality*. The inequality states that the total entropy cannot decrease over time. This is not enough information to enable scientists and mathematicians to identify the entropy function. Entropy is interesting to think about, but the information that the second law provides is more qualitative than quantitative. One prominent 20th-century mathematician and scientist who devoted much of his life to the study of thermodynamics, Clifford Truesdell, complained that whereas the claims of thermodynamics are often "grandiose," its applications are often "trivial."

Professor Truesdell enjoyed the overly dramatic statement, but if one did believe that the applications of thermodynamics were trivial at the beginning of the 20th century, one would probably agree with Truesdell's assessment, which was made near the midpoint of the century. The second law of thermodynamics, despite numerous attempts to reformulate it in the search for interesting applications, was still largely a qualitative statement. Meanwhile other areas of mathematics and physics were surging ahead.

In physics scientists had become very interested in discontinuous processes. A discontinuous process is one in which the physical properties of the material change in a way that can be reasonably modeled as "instantaneous." A common example of a discontinuous process is a shock wave. For example, the shock wave that is generated by a plane flying faster than sound causes an almost instantaneous jump in pressure and temperature as the shock wave moves through the air. The importance of understanding the effect of shock waves on the structure and handling of the plane and on the environment below became increasingly important as engineers sought ever-greater control over these powerful machines. Scientists learned to generate shock waves in wind tunnels and other devices to measure how the properties of the gas change as it passes from one side of the shock to the other.

Mathematically shock waves represent a new type of problem. In the 19th century scientists had developed mathematical models for phenomena that change gradually. The curves that represent changes in a physical system—for example, the temperature and pressure of a smoothly flowing gas—describe smooth contours. There are no corners or "clifflike" jumps in the graphs of these functions. Mathematically the smoothness of the curve is important, because when a curve varies smoothly all of the techniques of calculus can be brought to bear in the analysis of the curve and whatever it represents. By contrast the graphs of shock waves have sharp corners and jumps. Under these circumstances many of the techniques that are central to calculus cannot be used. Although calculus can be applied to the region on each side of the shock wave, it often does not work when applied to the shock itself. Of course the area near the shock wave is just the area that scientists and engineers most wanted to model.

Hypersonic flow. The shock wave is visible as lines trailing off the tip of the arrow-shaped object. (Courtesy of the Archives, California Institute of Technology)

The solution to the failure of the old ideas and techniques was to expand both the idea of a function and the techniques necessary to manipulate functions. This had to be done with care, however. Calculus had proven itself to be very useful, and no one was willing to abandon it. The key was to develop a new branch of mathematics that would extend rather than replace calculus. In this way calculus could be subsumed into a larger, more versatile structure.

Much of this new mathematics was first developed in the 1930s by a large group of highly creative mathematicians living in the former Soviet Union. The Soviet government was very generous in its support of the mathematical sciences. In many other areas of Soviet life political repression was more the rule than the exception, but in mathematics there was a great deal of intellectual freedom. Consequently a career in mathematics was a very attractive option for many intellectually curious Soviets, and many ambitious Soviet citizens availed themselves of the opportunity to excel mathematically. Mathematical research was carried out in most of the major cities and some smaller cities as well.

It was in these research centers—especially at those in Moscow and Leningrad (St. Petersburg)—that the concepts and techniques of a new and very expressive mathematical language were developed. When these new techniques were applied to the traditional functions, they yielded the traditional results. This was important because the traditional results were accurate when they existed. The new ideas and techniques, however, could be applied to a much larger class of functions, functions that could not be analyzed by using the techniques of the old calculus. The hope was that the new mathematics would be up to the task of analyzing the problems arising in the new physics.

It was in this environment that the Soviet mathematician Olga Oleinik (1925–2001) began her research into *discontinuous functions*—functions whose graphs exhibit breaks or jumps. Oleinik was a creative and unusually prolific mathematician. Born in Kiev, she received a Ph.D. from Moscow State University, one of the most important Soviet institutions of higher learning. Her thesis adviser, a man of whom she always spoke highly, was Ivan G.

Petrovsky (1901–73), an expert in the field of differential equations. His influence is apparent in much of Oleinik's work. After graduation Oleinik joined the faculty at Moscow State University and eventually became head of the department of differential equations. She wrote well over 300 research papers in mathematics as well as a number of books. In one of her best-known journal articles, "Discontinuous Solutions to Non-Linear Differential Equations," Oleinik investigated the mathematical properties of a class of conservation laws. We call these equations conservation laws because of their form, not because they are associated with any particular physical phenomena. To be sure, it is possible to associate some of the equations in the set of equations that Oleinik studied with specific physical phenomena, but this was not her goal. She was searching for general patterns, not specific solutions.

In her famous paper Oleinik studied the motion of a shock wave, but she immediately encountered a problem. The old calculus could not be used to study shock waves. Shock waves are discontinuous—their graphs have "clifflike" jumps. With traditional methods the equations that describe the shock have no solution. Under the new, generalized calculus, however, these same equations have too many solutions. In fact there are sometimes infinitely many solutions to a single equation. From a scientific point of view this is very undesirable. The goal of this type of mathematical analysis is to predict as precisely as possible what happens when we know the equation and the initial conditions of the system that we want to study. To say that, mathematically speaking, almost anything may happen to this system is to say very little that is useful, because in an experiment there are only room and time for one outcome to occur. Oleinik sought a criterion that would enable her to choose from the infinitely many solutions that *could* occur that one solution that *would* occur.

Oleinik's paper is famous in mathematical circles because she found a way to do just that. Her great insight was to identify what is now known as an entropy condition. This is a mathematical abstraction of the idea of entropy. She showed that though there might be infinitely many functions that *could* serve as valid solutions to the type of conservation law that she studied, there was only one function that satisfied both the conservation law and her entropy condition. This discovery is an important breakthrough in mathematical physics because it restores the concept that to each properly posed differential equation there corresponds exactly one solution. It is essentially the mathematical version of the idea of cause and effect. It has also been the most important attempt to date to use a mathematical formulation of the entropy concept in an essential way.

9

NATURAL LAWS AND RANDOMNESS

Since the Renaissance mathematicians have been concerned with the laws of cause and effect. That is, they have sought to employ the mathematical expression of these laws so that for any particular phenomenon there exists a one-to-one relationship between each cause and each effect. Their goal has been to solve the following simple-sounding problem: Given a unique cause, predict the unique effect. Many phenomena are well suited to this type of mathematical analysis, but there are also situations in which this approach fails. When this happens scientists have learned to rephrase the problem in the language of probability. One modern version of this idea can be described as follows: Given a unique cause, predict the most probable effect. A more general version of the problem is: Given the most probable cause, predict the most probable effect. These types of probabilistic problems are now a fundamental part of science, but this is a fairly recent development.

Mathematicians and scientists have long sought to incorporate ideas from the theory of probability in science. Until the second half of the 19th century, however, most attempts to use probability theory in science involved quantifying the ignorance of the investigator. Often implicit in the work of these early scientists was the belief that the more they knew, the less they would need the theory of probability. Philosophically they believed that if one knew enough, one would not need probability at all. They viewed probability as a stopgap measure—a theory of errors, the goal of which was to locate the most probable "true" value given a set of somewhat inaccurate measurements. As errors were eliminated, these scholars believed, the need for probability theory would decrease accordingly. This concept of probability theory stems from the fact that these scientists believed that there was nothing essentially random in what they studied. In fact many of the best scientists, such as the French mathematician and physicist Pierre Simon Laplace, explicitly rejected the existence of anything truly random in nature.

One of the first scientists to develop a scientific theory that uses randomness in an essential way was the Austrian monk, botanist, and geneticist Gregor Mendel (1822–84). He began to investigate the genetics of heredity in the 1850s and 1860s. The results of his painstaking research are summarized in what are now known as Mendel's laws of heredity. Mendel published an essentially complete, and in many ways an essentially correct, theory of heredity in 1866. The journal in which he published his ideas could be found in many of the major libraries of Europe, but his work attracted virtually no attention at all until 1900, when his results were rediscovered by another generation of researchers. This is a reflection of how far ahead of his time Mendel, in fact, was. His ideas were too far removed from the scientific orthodoxy of his day to draw any converts at all. It was not for lack of trying. Mendel corresponded, for example, with a distinguished botanist, Karl Wilhelm von Nägeli, but von Nägeli, like others in the field, completely missed the significance of Mendel's discoveries.

Mendel had an unusual background for someone who is now recognized as a brilliant researcher. He received two years of education in the sciences at the Philosophical Institute of Olmütz, located in what is now the Czech Republic in the city of Olomouc. (During Mendel's life Olomouc was part of the Austro-Hungarian Empire.) After he left the Philosophical Institute Mendel entered a monastery. He later became a priest and subsequently enrolled at the University of Vienna for an additional two years; there he studied mathematics and science. His aptitude in science was not immediately apparent. When Mendel attempted to become licensed as a teacher, he failed the test, scoring particularly poorly in the natural sciences.

Undeterred, he began his self-directed experiments in heredity in 1854.

To appreciate better the magnitude of Mendel's insight into genetics, knowing something about the scientific theory of inheritance that prevailed throughout his lifetime is useful. Sometimes called blended inheritance or inheritance by blood, this theory is meant to account for the fact that sometimes the characteristics of the offspring are intermediate between those of the two parents. The name of the theory stems from the idea that an individual's traits are carried in the blood, and that the traits of

Gregor Mendel. Randomness is an integral part of his theory of heredity. (Topham/The Image Works)

the offspring are the result of the blended blood of the parents. By analogy, if we use red dye to color water in one glass and yellow dye to color water in a second glass, we obtain orange water if we mix the water in the two glasses together. Orange is the color that is intermediate between the two "parent" colors.

Casual inspection shows that this theory is false. There are many traits that do not blend. One of the parents may have a particular trait—blue eyes, for example—that is not apparent in any of the offspring. More telling, a trait may appear in the offspring even though neither parent exhibits it. There is another, logical reason for rejecting the idea of blended inheritance. If the traits of the offspring were, in fact, midway between those of the parents, then some of the uniqueness of each parent generation would be lost and no new unique traits would be gained since the new traits were "blended" from the old. As a consequence each generation would exhibit less variability than the preceding one. After a few generations all individuals would be identical.

(To return to the colored-water analogy, if we had a shelf full of glasses, each containing a different color of water, and the different color waters were mixed together two at a time, it would not be long before the water in all the glasses was precisely the same color.) But variability persists. The existence of easy-to-recognize individuals in most species of plants and animals proves that individual traits are maintained from generation to generation. Blending inheritance cannot be correct. Recognizing that something is incorrect, however, offers little insight into what is true.

Mendel was living at a monastery when he began to search for the truth about inheritance. He studied how several easy-to-identify traits in pea plants were inherited, but his discoveries went well beyond these plants. Implicit in his approach is the belief that the mechanisms that control heredity in pea plants control heredity in other organisms as well.

Mendel's approach was exhaustive; it must have been personally exhausting as well. His goal was a quantitative one. He wanted to count the traits exhibited by thousands of individuals over multiple generations in the hope of finding a pattern that would reveal the mechanism of heredity. There are several practical advantages to the use of pea plants. First, a garden full of such plants can easily yield a large number of individuals for study. Second, pea plants are usually self-pollinating, so all the genes of the offspring are generally inherited from the one parent. This makes it easier to deduce what genes the parent does or does not have by examining the appearance of the offspring. No variability in some trait of the offspring is a good indication that the parent has only one version of a particular gene. (This situation is often described by saying the parent is *purebred*—which is just another way of saying that the parent has little genetic variation.) Conversely knowledge of the parent's genetic makeup often makes deducing the genetic makeup of the offspring simple. Third, most of the cross-pollination that did occur in his garden setting could be attributed directly to Mendel's own efforts rather than the randomizing action of insects. Finally, pea plants exhibit easy-to-observe variation in a number of distinct traits. For Mendel the pea plant was ideal.

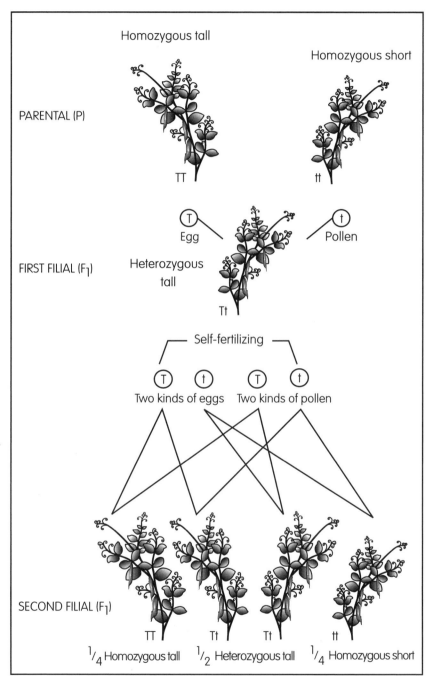

Diagram illustrating Gregor Mendel's laws of heredity

Mendel tracked a number of traits from generation to generation. Among these traits were flower color (purple vs. white), plant height (tall vs. short), and seed shape (round vs. wrinkled). His method was to cross two purebred individuals and observe how a trait, or combination of traits, would be expressed in succeeding generations. For example, when Mendel crossed a purebred plant that could only produce white flowers with a purebred plant that could only produce purple flowers, he noticed that the first generation exhibited only purple flowers. Similarly when he crossed a purebred tall plant with a purebred short plant, the first generation after the cross was composed of all tall individuals. This is almost an argument for the theory of blended inheritance, because it appears that the variation between plants had been reduced through the act of pollination.

Mendel described the situation by saying that purple was dominant to white and that white was recessive to purple. Similarly he said that tall was dominant to short and short was recessive to tall. The interesting event occurred during the next generation: When Mendel allowed the tall, purple hybrids to self-pollinate, some individuals in the next generation had purple flowers and others had white. Some were tall and some were short. This clearly disproved the theory that the traits had blended, and to Mendel it showed that heredity had a particulate nature—that is, there were individual bits that acted together to produce a trait. Combine the bits in a different way and the visible traits of the plant changed accordingly. In particular the bits were not destroyed in the act of creating a new individual. They were preserved from one generation to the next. Today we call these bits of information genes.

Not satisfied with a qualitative explanation for the mechanism of heredity, Mendel found a quantitative explanation. He hypothesized that each trait that he studied was governed by two genes. Each parent contributed one of the genes. The dominant gene for each trait determined how the trait was expressed. An individual that inherited a dominant gene from each parent displayed the dominant trait, but so did any individual that received one dominant gene and one recessive gene. Again the trait that appeared in the individual was determined solely by the dominant gene. If, on the other hand, no dominant gene was present—if the individual had two copies of a recessive gene—then the recessive trait was expressed.

This theory accounts for the absence of white flowers in the first generation after a purebred plant with purple flowers is crossed with a purebred one with white flowers. Each of the offspring has one gene for purple flowers and one gene for white flowers. Because purple is dominant to white, the result is all purple flowers. The same can be said for the absence of short plants in the first generation following the cross. Each member of the first generation of offspring carries one gene for tall plant height and one gene for short plant height. Significantly each member of this generation of pea plants carries two sources of future variation that cannot be directly observed: one gene for white flowers and one gene for short plant height.

There is considerable variation in the second generation of flowers after the cross. In fact this generation shows more variability in appearance than either of the two preceding generations. There are tall plants with purple flowers and tall plants with white flowers. There are short plants with purple flowers and short plants with white flowers. Moreover, because pea plants are usually self-pollinating, the source of this variation can only be found in the genetic makeup of the individuals in the first generation after the initial cross. (This is called the first filial generation, or F_1 generation.) When Mendel counted, he found that almost exactly three-quarters of the plants in the second generation after the cross—this is usually called the F_2 generation—had purple flowers and one-quarter had white flowers. Similarly almost exactly three-quarters of the plants in the F_2 generation were tall and one-quarter were short.

This type of situation is easy to duplicate by flipping two coins. Imagine flipping a penny and a quarter. If either comes up heads we keep both. If both come up tails we lose both. What are the possibilities? They can both come up heads, and that is the first way to win. The penny can come up heads and the quarter can come up tails. That is the second way to win. The quarter can come up heads and the penny can come up tails. That is the third way to win. Finally, they can both come up tails and we lose. If we play this game a large number of times, we can expect to win three-quarters of the time. We can expect to lose one-quarter of the time. These are the ratios Mendel observed.

Mendel also discovered an interesting pattern related to the way flower color and plant height were associated. He noticed that about nine-sixteenths of all the plants in the F_2 generation were tall and purple, about three-sixteenths were tall and white, about three-sixteenths were short and purple, and about one-sixteenth were short and white.

This situation can also be duplicated by using coin flips. Suppose that we play two games simultaneously. One game is the quarter–penny game described. The second game is played with a nickel and a dime, but according to the same rules as the quarter–penny game. The result is that we win all the coins about nine-sixteenths of the time. We win the quarter and penny and lose the nickel and dime about three-sixteenths of the time. We lose the quarter and penny and win the nickel and dime three-sixteenths of the time, and finally, we lose all four coins one-sixteenth of the time.

Mendel concluded that the gene that the offspring inherited for flower color had no effect on which plant height gene was passed along. Nor did the plant height gene affect the inheritance of the gene for flower color. The genes for flower color and plant height were *segregating* along the same rules that governed our coin flipping game.

Mendel was right. There was much that he did not know, of course. He did not know about deoxyribonucleic acid (DNA). Nor did he know about chromosomes, which are large structures along which the genes are organized. But for the traits that he analyzed his conclusions were correct. In some general way he understood the cause of the variation—what we now call genes—and he understood the effect—the traits that he observed in the appearance of the plants. His conclusions were, however, unlike those of the scientists who preceded him. Unlike Newton, Lavoisier, and Clausius, all of whom could predict an individual effect for each individual cause, Mendel often could not predict the appearance of *individual* offspring on the basis of knowledge of the genetic background of the parent. If there were many offspring he could, with reasonable accuracy, predict the *frequency* with which a particular trait would appear, but that was the extent of it. The act of inheritance—the precise collection of alleles that are passed from parent to offspring during the act of reproduction—is a random phenomenon. Mendel had uncovered not just the laws of heredity, but also a law of nature that could be expressed only in the language of probability. Mendel's laws of inheritance depended on chance.

Today scientists know considerably more about heredity than Mendel could have dreamed. They know the chemical structure of the DNA molecule. For several types of organisms they know how the individual genes are organized on the chromosomes. They sometimes understand how the chemical information carried by the DNA molecule is expressed in the individual organism, and they understand the mechanism by which the genes are sorted and passed from one generation to the next. None of this, however, has enabled them to eliminate the role of chance. Given a field of pea plants with known characteristics, the appearance of the next generation of offspring can still only be described via the language of probability. Chance is an integral part of the laws of heredity.

Population Genetics

In the hundred or so years since Mendel's work was rediscovered and genetics became an important area of scientific research, the field has divided into two distinct branches. One branch of genetics, called molecular genetics, is in the field of chemistry. In this discipline scientists are concerned with the precise chemical makeup of genes, their physical location on the chromosomes, and their biochemical function. This is an important way of understanding genetics, and at present it is the approach most often described in the popular press. The other approach to genetics is called population genetics.

Population genetics is, in spirit, closer to the approach first adopted by Mendel himself. As its name implies, population genetics is the study of how genes and combinations of genes are distributed in a population. It is also the study of how and why gene frequencies change over the course of time. The physical characteristics of a group of organisms are determined in large measure by the genetic makeup of the group, that is, the types of genes present, their frequency, and the ways they are grouped together in individuals. The genetic makeup of the group determines its response to its environment, and its response to its environment determines the genetic makeup of future generations. Changes in gene frequencies occur *between* generations, not within them.

Individual organisms can be important in the study of population genetics, but always in a very restricted way. Individuals cannot change their genes. Almost always the genes an individual organism is born with are the genes with which that organism dies. Furthermore most mutations, or spontaneous genetic changes, that do occur over the course of an individual's life are not passed on to the next generation, because most mutations do not occur in the reproductive cells. The individual's genetic contribution to the next generation is generally made from the set of genes with which that individual was born. What is of interest to population geneticists is the "fitness" of each individual organism to transmit those genes. In fact, from the point of view of population genetics, reproductive fitness determines the importance of the individual. Each individual organism is modeled as the mechanism through which genes interact with the environment.

Because molecular genetics and population genetics are so different in concept, it should be no surprise that the tools used to investigate them are often different as well. There are exceptions, of course, but molecular genetics is generally studied in the lab. By contrast questions in population genetics are often better expressed in the language of mathematics. Population geneticists often seek to model mathematically how each species changes in the context of its ever-changing environment.

The first important law of population genetics was published in 1908, less than a decade after Mendel's work was rediscovered. It is called the Hardy-Weinberg law, and it was discovered by the British mathematician Godfrey Harold Hardy (1877–1947) and the German physician Wilhelm Weinberg (1862–1937). Hardy and Weinberg independently discovered the theorem that bears their names. This theorem is fundamental to the subject of population genetics, but it seems to have been less important to one of its discoverers. Hardy downplayed the importance of the result. His objections were, at bottom, probably based on aesthetics. G. H. Hardy was a self-described "pure" mathematician; one of his best-known books is *A Course in Pure Mathematics*. He liked to describe his work as having no value outside the field of mathematics, but the Hardy-Weinberg law is an exception to this rule. Later more of his discoveries would find important applications outside mathematics, a fact that would surely have left him chagrined. Weinberg's feelings about his discovery are not known.

The Hardy-Weinberg law is, to be sure, a counterintuitive kind of result. It is a sort of conservation law. It states that under certain conditions gene frequencies are conserved from one generation to the next. Unlike the conservation laws of classical physics, however, the conditions that guarantee that gene frequencies are conserved are never satisfied.

In the years immediately following the rediscovery of Mendelian genetics, there was a great deal of excitement about how the new ideas could be used to describe genetic change. It is apparent from looking at everything from fossils to the breeding records of livestock that the characteristics that define a species of organisms can and do change over time. Sometimes the changes are small and sometimes the changes are very large. Mendel's ideas about the particulate nature of inheritance suggest the possibility of quantifying changes in heredity as changes in the statistical distribution of genes. In theory, at least, the slow accumulation of changes in gene frequencies could, over the course of many generations, turn wild ponies into large Belgian draft horses or into small Shetland ponies. Populations of fish might change into populations of amphibians. This is not what Hardy and Weinberg showed, however. Their instinct was, instead, to examine the conditions under which change could *not* occur.

Hardy and Weinberg imagined a population of organisms, all of which belong to the same species, that satisfies the following conditions: (1) The population must be very large. (2) Reproduction occurs in a random fashion. (3) There is no migration into or out of the population in question. (4) There are no differential survival rates. (5) The number of offspring produced does not vary from individual to individual or between reproducing pairs of individuals. (6) The genes do not mutate; that is, they do not change spontaneously from one form to another. Under these conditions Hardy and Weinberg mathematically proved that gene frequencies are *stable:* That is, the frequencies themselves are conserved from one generation to the next. Any population that satisfies the Hardy-Weinberg conditions is said to be in *equilibrium.*

To understand the importance of this first and fundamental law of population genetics, it is important to understand the meaning of the assumptions on which the conclusion is based. The assumption that the population is very large means that random fluctuations play no role in the transmission of genes. To understand why, consider the coin-flipping problem again. It is common knowledge that the odds of flipping a head are 50/50; when we flip a coin a head is as likely to result from the flip as a tail. It does not follow, however, that if a coin is flipped several times we see as many heads as tails. In fact, if we flip the coin an odd number of times, we are guaranteed to see a difference in the number of heads versus the number of tails. Less obvious is that if we flip the coin many times it is highly unlikely that we will ever see exactly as many heads as tails, even when the coin is flipped an even number of times. What happens instead is that the quotient formed by the total number of heads divided by the total number of flips approaches the number 1/2 as the number of flips becomes very large. This much is "guaranteed." In a small set of flips, however, even this quotient is unsteady. For example if we flip a coin three times, there is a 25 percent chance that the three flips will be either all heads or all tails.

Mathematically the genetics problem is exactly the same as the coin-flipping problem. Suppose one parent has two different forms of the same gene—different forms of the same gene are *alleles.* We call the alleles carried by our imaginary parent *a* and *A*. Suppose that this parent has three offspring. There is a 25 percent chance that all the offspring will inherit the *a* allele from that parent or that they will all inherit the *A* allele. In the first case the *A* allele is lost in the sense that it is not passed on to the next generation. In the second case the *a* allele is lost. In a large population these random fluctuations balance out, but in a small population there is a good chance that small random fluctuations can lead to measurable and permanent changes in gene frequency throughout the entire population only because of the "luck of the draw."

The second assumption of the Hardy-Weinberg law is that reproduction occurs randomly in the sense that no isolated subpopulations occur within the larger population. A small "subcommunity" of organisms that for several generations reproduces in isolation from the main body of organisms, for example, begins to show statistical changes in gene frequency that are due to the random fluctuations described in the preceding paragraph.

Third, migration into or out of the population can be expected to change the genetic makeup of the population. A flow of individuals out of the main population leads to the loss of specific genes and possibly a change in the statistical distribution of the genes. A flow of individuals into the main population can also disrupt the statistical makeup of the gene pool. It may even cause new genes to be introduced into the population we are considering.

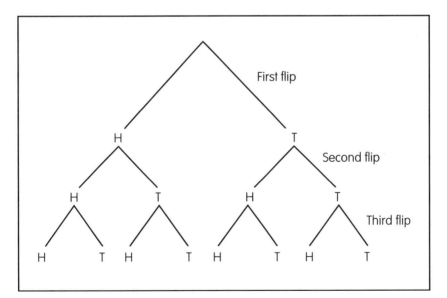

There are eight possible paths from the top of the diagram to the bottom. Each path represents a different sequence of coin flips. The paths HHH and TTT represent one-fourth or 25 percent of all possible sequences.

Fourth, "There are no differential survival rates or reproduction rates" means that no allele of any gene can be more advantageous to the survival of any individual than any other allele. If an individual does not survive to reproductive age, then that individual cannot be expected to reproduce.

Fifth, every individual that reproduces must produce as many offspring as any other individual. For example, if one plant produces only a few seeds and another plant of the same species produces hundreds or even thousands of seeds, then the genes of the second plant will probably be overrepresented in the next generation compared with the genes of the first plant, and this, of course, is a change in the gene frequencies present from one generation to the next.

Finally, Hardy and Weinberg assert that in order for gene frequencies to remain unchanged from one generation to the next, mutations cannot occur. Mutations are spontaneous, random changes in a gene. If we imagine a gene as a single very long word, a mutation would be the addition, deletion, or substitution of one or more letters within the word. A mutation can improve the function of the gene, but because they occur randomly, most mutations either are harmful or have no effect on gene function.

There does not exist a single population anywhere on Earth that satisfies all of these restrictions. There are some populations that are large enough so that random fluctuations in gene frequencies play no role, but, for example, mutations and differential reproduction rates are present in virtually every population. As a consequence the conditions for the validity of the Hardy-Weinberg equations are never satisfied in practice. It may seem, then, that the Hardy-Weinberg law is useless, but this is not the case.

Variations in gene frequencies over time can be measured. Sometimes they can be measured with great precision. For example, some scientists take tissue samples from numerous individuals and then analyze the DNA in each sample. Sometimes this is not possible and cruder measures, such as changes in the appearance of fossils, are studied. Each type of measurement can tell us something about the speed with which gene frequencies are changing. As soon as scientists obtain information on the types of change that are

Though it is difficult to estimate accurately the amount of genetic change that has occurred over time from a study of the fossil record, the set of all fossils constitutes some of the strongest evidence that large changes have occurred. (Science Museum, London/Topham-HIP/The Image Works)

occurring as well as their speed, it becomes possible, in theory, to associate the observed changes with one or more of the conditions in the Hardy-Weinberg hypothesis. The list is important, because Weinberg and Hardy proved that *if* the conditions on the list are satisfied *then* gene frequencies are stable; it follows that *if* the frequencies are not stable *then* not all the conditions are satisfied.

The Hardy-Weinberg law also points out the existence of another type of genetic phenomenon: Some genes are not adaptive. They can in fact injure the carrier. Organisms born with these genes may exhibit developmental problems. Sometimes they even show a higher rate of mortality. Because these genes can injure the carrier, it is reasonable to expect their frequency over time to decline. The carrier is, after all, less likely to transmit these genes to the next generation. This is true now, but it was also true 1,000 generations ago, a fact that raises questions: Why haven't these genes already been eliminated from the species in which they occur? How did they reach their present frequency? There is usually no clear answer to either of these questions, but the Hardy-Weinberg law can offer some broad hints.

In a large population if the only effect of the gene is deleterious, and if the gene has always been deleterious, then it should be either absent or extremely rare. Because this is not always the case, it is necessary to look more closely at the situation. The classic example of a gene with more than one effect is the gene responsible for the disease sickle-cell anemia.

Sickle-cell anemia is a disease of the red blood cells. It is painful, difficult to treat, and currently incurable, and it lasts as long as the person with the disease lives. It is a genetic disease caused by a single gene. The gene responsible for sickle-cell anemia has two forms, or alleles, a "normal" form and the form responsible for the disease. We let the letter A represent the normal form of the gene. The letter a represents the allele responsible for the sickle cell.

Sickle-cell anemia arose in human populations exposed to high rates of malaria. Individuals who possess two copies of the normal gene are especially susceptible to malaria. Malaria is a deadly disease and people with two normal genes are especially susceptible to its effects. Individuals with two copies of the sickle-cell gene have the disorder sickle-cell anemia, which is also a serious health problem. The interesting case occurs when an individual has one normal gene and one sickle-cell gene. In this case the individual is especially resistant to the effects of malaria. When the gene for sickle-cell anemia is rare in the population, it is a tremendous advantage not just to the individual who carries one copy of the gene but to the offspring of that individual as well. The fact that a gene is rare means that the individual with just one sickle-cell gene probably reproduces with an individual with two normal genes. As a consequence they can expect that on average 50 percent of their children will have one copy of the sickle-cell gene and one normal gene; on average 50 percent of their children will be resistant to the disease malaria. Under the circumstances we should expect to see the frequency of the gene for sickle-cell anemia increase in the population because those with two normal genes are less likely to reproduce successfully.

The complication arises as the gene becomes more and more frequent in the population. In this case it becomes increasingly likely that two individuals, each with one copy of the normal gene and one copy of the sickle-cell gene, will reproduce. Under these circumstances, 50 percent of their children are, on average, still resistant to malaria, but on average 25 percent of their children have sickle-cell anemia, and sickle-cell anemia, like malaria, is a significant cause of death.

The gene for sickle cell is especially common in areas of Africa where malaria rates are high. Many people in North America, South America, and the Caribbean can trace their ancestry to these areas of Africa. They still sometimes carry the gene for sickle cell, but now there is no advantage in carrying the gene; they live in an environment where malaria never occurs.

If scientists had not uncovered the role of the gene in the environment in Africa where it arose, the presence of the gene would be impossible to explain. In Canada, for example, where there has never been any malaria, the gene is clearly disadvantageous. There the gene is present for historical reasons. In recent times many Africans have immigrated to Canada, and historically there were many slaves who escaped their mistreatment in the United States by escaping to Canada, where slavery was illegal. Sickle-cell anemia is one example of a genetic disease that can be explained only through science *and* history. There are other diseases whose presence can be explained similarly. Scientists cannot, however, account for all genetic diseases by using a sickle-cell model. This may be because there are other factors at work or because the historical reasons that might account for the presence of the disease have yet to be uncovered. The Hardy-Weinberg law does not offer us any guidance about the specifics, but it does offer us a way of framing our questions about population genetics.

The Limits of Predictability

A great deal of mathematical modeling has been done to try to quantify how changes in gene frequencies are related to each of the conditions on which the Hardy-Weinberg law is based.

Meteorology is concerned with large-scale motions of the atmosphere. The mathematical models derived from the study of weather are often expressed in the language of probability theory. (Courtesy of National Oceanic and Atmospheric Administration/Department of Commerce)

Although the Hardy-Weinberg conditions seem straightforward, they are not. They can be violated in various ways that are not especially obvious. For example, scientists have sought to answer the question, How large a population is so large that the gene frequencies are not affected by random fluctuations? Although this question seems as if it should have a single number for an answer, it does not. For example, 500 individuals may, under some circumstances, be sufficient to even out random fluctuations for five generations, but that same population under the same circumstances is probably not large enough to ensure stability over 500 generations. Over the course of 500 generations there are many more opportunities for unlikely events to occur.

One more example of a situation in which a hypothesis of the Hardy-Weinberg law is violated: Mutations are random changes in genes, and so far we have described them as if they occur at a uniform rate. Sometimes this is just what happens. (Mutation rates can be measured by the number of spontaneous changes occurring in the DNA of an organism per unit of time.) Scientists have discovered, however, that certain species of organisms have genes that affect the mutation rate itself. This means that individual organisms can carry a "mutation gene" that significantly accelerates the rate at which changes occur in the organism's DNA. Predicting the effect or even the existence of such genes can be very difficult indeed.

For many years population geneticists had to content themselves with studying extremely simple model problems. "Real-life" problems involving actual populations were far too difficult to understand. More complicated problems were often mathematically intractable, but even when this was not the case, the measurements on which the solutions depended were too difficult to make accurately. As a consequence the connection between theory and practice was weak.

Change is gradual. It depends on several factors. One factor that made progress possible was better information about genetics and the mechanisms involved in heredity. As scientists acquired more information, they were better able to predict mutation rates and the way that individual genes function as part of the complement of genes that make up the individual and the species. The second factor that affected progress was computer technology. Computers enabled scientists and mathematicians to solve mathematical problems that had previously proved too difficult. Scientists also developed technology that enables them to sample the DNA of the species of interest directly. This gives them better information about current gene frequencies and it also makes it possible to measure changes in gene frequency more accurately. All of this was important, but it is a measure of the difficulty of the problems involved that in many ways progress has remained incremental. Today scientists are sometimes able to make reasonably accurate short-term predictions about changes in the genetic variability of a population of organisms. However, because of the enormous uncertainties involved, the accuracy of these predictions quickly decays as the period under consideration increases.

With all of these qualifications about the difficulty of applying the laws of population genetics, it may seem that the physical sciences have made far more progress in their ability to predict nature than have population geneticists. The situation is, however, somewhat more complicated. To be sure, there are many situations in which physical scientists have now become accustomed to making many highly accurate predictions about the state of some physical system far in the future. No one, for example, is especially surprised when a space vehicle is launched toward some distant planet and arrives just as it was predicted to arrive months or even years before launch. In fact, we tend to be surprised when this does not happen. There is, as we have already pointed out, no theory or technique in the field of population genetics that enables scientists to make the same sorts of extraordinary predictions.

A major difference between population genetics and classical physics is related to the role of chance. Newton, Lavoisier, and Clausius were able to develop very satisfying theories—theories that can be used to make accurate predictions about future events—without any appeal to ideas of chance and randomness. Mendel, by contrast, was unable to form even an elementary theory of heredity without incorporating ideas of randomness in his theory. It would be incorrect to assume, however, that the laws of probability have not also found a home in the physical sciences.

There seem to be inherent limits on predictability even in the physical sciences. Today there are aspects of the physical sciences that *cannot* be expressed without concepts taken from the field of probability. Sometimes probability is required because the phenomenon to be studied seems to be fundamentally random. This is the case with turbulent fluids. Fluids that are turbulent—rushing water and rushing air are two examples—currently defy precise prediction, and some scientists believe that they always will. It is certainly true that the best that can now be done is to predict "most probable" values. One can, for example, predict the most probable range of velocities that would appear at some point at some time in a turbulent fluid moving under a given set of conditions. Accuracy in this sense means predicting a narrow range of velocities with a high probability. Sometimes scientists have been successful in this regard; often they have not.

The study of random phenomena is one of a number of disciplines in which physical scientists use probability theory in an essential way. Another situation arises when scientists cannot accurately measure the state of the system in which they have an interest. They may feel confident that they have the right equations—equations that allow them to predict an effect provided that they know a cause—but the equations themselves are never enough. To solve a differential equation fully—recall that the laws of nature are generally expressed in terms of differential equations—one must have more than the equation.

Scientists also need information about the state of the system. Sometimes this information is unavailable. It is sometimes the case that scientists are unsure about the precise state of the system at *any* time and that they have no method for eliminating this uncertainty. Scientists have, for example, developed a wide variety of predictions about motions occurring deep within the Earth. (These predictions are generally made with the help of the equations of continuity, the law of conservation of momentum, and the law of conservation of energy.) The problem is that their predictions depend on certain assumptions about what is actually occurring deep inside Earth right now; no one has access to this information. Sometimes the devices necessary to make the measurements have yet to be constructed. Sometimes it is not clear even in theory how one might construct such a device. These uncertainties are reflected in the existence of several competing theories about the dynamics of the processes that occur deep within our planet.

Uncertainty in any science has never proved a barrier to the development of new theories or the making of new predictions. It is reflected, instead, in a general lack of confidence in the validity of apparently correct predictions. If a prediction turns out to be reasonably accurate—and no theory in population genetics or in the theory of turbulent fluids, for example, has proved to be more

GENETIC COUNSELING

There are a host of deadly genes present in the human gene pool. These genes are generally recessive. (Genes that are deadly and dominant always eliminate the carrier. If this occurs before the carrier is able to reproduce, then that gene is not transferred to the next generation and is lost forever.) Furthermore, most of the really harmful genes exist at very low frequencies, because at higher frequencies the carriers are more likely to encounter one another and produce offspring that are not viable. Nonviable offspring again eliminate the genes that they carry. Since there is generally no "penalty" for simply being the carrier of any recessive gene, deadly or not, these genes simply persist in the general population in accordance with the Hardy-Weinberg law. Many of us, for example, carry some recessive genes that would be very harmful or fatal if expressed.

It does occasionally happen that a couple has reason to believe that one or both of them are carriers for some specific harmful genetic trait.

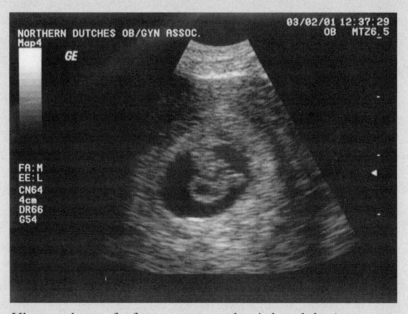

Ultrasound scan of a fetus at seven weeks. As knowledge increases, we will be faced with situations and decisions unimagined even a generation ago. (Maya Barnes/The Image Works)

The clue can be family history: Perhaps a relative has exhibited this trait, or the couple already has a child who exhibits the trait. Another indicator might be the couple's ethnic background. There are some populations who, because of long periods of social or geographic isolation, have accumulated particular genetic diseases at unusually high frequencies.

Genetic counselors are individuals with an education in genetics, especially population genetics, as well as counseling, probability, and statistics. It is their job to help couples thinking about having children evaluate the risk in doing so. They approach their task with the latest statistical information about gene frequencies in the "general" population as well as information about gene frequencies among specific subgroups. They must be conversant with the medical characteristics of a host of genetic diseases. From this information they can estimate the probability that a particular couple will produce a child with the trait of interest.

What is to be done with this information? Risk, in the end, is in the eye of the beholder. Although it is possible to evaluate risk, the meaning of the risk—and in particular the determination of whether or not to risk having a child with a particular trait—is always a matter for the couple to decide. Although certain tests can determine whether an individual is a carrier of a particular gene, there is no test that can tell an individual what is the "right" course of action for him or her. This is where the genetic counselor's counseling skills are required.

The job of genetic counselor is becoming increasingly important as information about human genetics increases. As knowledge proliferates, couples are faced with increasingly complicated decisions about what, if anything, they should do to control the genetic makeup of the children they may have in the future. The complications arise because with increasingly sophisticated technology, it is not only possible to know more about the child before it is born; it is also possible to do more to the child before it is born. Operations can now be performed on the fetus, and the potential for genetic manipulation is on the horizon. As the number of options increases, so does the complexity of the decisions with which couples will be faced.

than "reasonably accurate"—there is still the question of whether the agreement is the result of a coincidence or whether the prediction displays real insight. The answer to this type of question is usually not clear. When scientists are interested in studying "random" phenomena, either they are forced to discuss the most likely "effect" of a given "cause," or they abandon the notion of cause and effect entirely and instead search for correlations between one data set and another. Rather than being mutually exclusive, the philosophy of cause and effect that is so characteristic of classical physics and the probabilistic analysis that is characteristic of population genetics are now just two alternative, complementary ways of perceiving the same phenomenon.

CHRONOLOGY

ca. 3000 B.C.E.
Hieroglyphic numerals are in use in Egypt.

ca. 2500 B.C.E.
Construction of the Great Pyramid of Khufu takes place.

ca. 2400 B.C.E.
An almost complete system of positional notation is in use in Mesopotamia.

ca. 1800 B.C.E.
The Code of Hammurabi is promulgated.

ca. 1650 B.C.E.
The Egyptian scribe Ahmes copies what is now known as the Ahmes (or Rhind) papyrus from an earlier version of the same document.

ca. 1200 B.C.E.
The Trojan War is fought.

ca. 740 B.C.E.
Homer composes the *Odyssey* and the *Iliad*, his epic poems about the Trojan War.

ca. 585 B.C.E.
Thales of Miletus carries out his research into geometry, marking the beginning of mathematics as a deductive science.

ca. 540 B.C.E.
Pythagoras of Samos establishes the Pythagorean school of philosophy.

ca. 500 B.C.E.
Rod numerals are in use in China.

ca. 420 B.C.E.

Zeno of Elea proposes his philosophical paradoxes.

ca. 399 B.C.E.

Socrates dies.

ca. 360 B.C.E.

Eudoxus, author of the method of exhaustion, carries out his research into mathematics.

ca. 350 B.C.E.

The Greek mathematician Menaechmus writes an important work on conic sections.

ca. 347 B.C.E.

Plato dies.

332 B.C.E.

Alexandria, Egypt, center of Greek mathematics, is established.

ca. 300 B.C.E.

Euclid of Alexandria writes *Elements*, one of the most influential mathematics books of all time.

ca. 260 B.C.E.

Aristarchus of Samos discovers a method for computing the ratio of the Earth-Moon distance to the Earth-Sun distance.

ca. 230 B.C.E.

Eratosthenes of Cyrene computes the circumference of Earth.

Apollonius of Perga writes *Conics*.

Archimedes of Syracuse writes *The Method, Equilibrium of Planes*, and other works.

206 B.C.E.

The Han dynasty is established; Chinese mathematics flourishes.

ca. C.E. 150

Ptolemy of Alexandria writes *Almagest*, the most influential astronomy text of antiquity.

ca. C.E. 250

Diophantus of Alexandria writes *Arithmetica*, an important step forward for algebra.

ca. 320

Pappus of Alexandria writes his *Collection*, one of the last influential Greek mathematical treatises.

415

The death of the Alexandrian philosopher and mathematician Hypatia marks the end of the Greek mathematical tradition.

ca. 476

The astronomer and mathematician Aryabhata is born; Indian mathematics flourishes.

ca. 630

The Hindu mathematician and astronomer Brahmagupta writes *Brahma-sphuta-siddhānta*, which contains a description of place-value notation.

641

The Library of Alexandria is burned.

ca. 775

Scholars in Baghdad begin to translate Hindu and Greek works into Arabic.

ca. 830

Mohammed ibn-Mūsā al-Khwārizmī writes *Hisāb al-jabr wa'l muqābala*, a new approach to algebra.

833

Al-Ma'mūn, founder of the House of Wisdom in Baghdad (now Iraq), dies.

ca. 840

The Jainist mathematician Mahavira writes *Ganita Sara Samgraha*, an important mathematical textbook.

1071

William the Conqueror quells the last of the English rebellions.

1086

An intensive survey of the wealth of England is carried out and summarized in the tables and lists of the *Domesday Book*.

1123

Omar Khayyám, author of *Al-jabr w'al muqābala* and the *Rubáiyát*, the last great classical Islamic mathematician, dies.

ca. 1144

Bhaskara II writes the *Lilavati* and the *Vija-Ganita*, two of the last great works in the classical Indian mathematical tradition.

ca. 1202

Leonardo of Pisa (Fibonacci), author of *Liber Abaci*, arrives in Europe from Africa, where his father worked.

1360

Nicholas Oresme, a French mathematician and Roman Catholic bishop, represents distance as the area beneath a velocity line.

1471

The German artist Albrecht Dürer is born.

1482

Leonardo da Vinci begins to record his diaries.

ca. 1541

Niccolò Fontana, an Italian mathematician, also known as Tartaglia, discovers a general method for factoring third-degree algebraic equations.

1543

Copernicus publishes *De Revolutionibus*, marking the start of the Copernican revolution.

1545

Girolamo Cardano, an Italian mathematician and physician, publishes *Ars Magna*, marking the beginning of modern algebra. Later he publishes *Liber de Ludo Aleae*, the first book on probability.

ca. 1554

Sir Walter Raleigh, an explorer, adventurer, and amateur mathematician and patron of mathematician Thomas Harriot, is born.

1579

François Viète, a French mathematician, publishes *Canon Mathematicus*, marking the beginning of modern algebraic notation.

1585

The Dutch mathematician and engineer Simon Stevin publishes "La disme."

1609

Johannes Kepler, the author of Kepler's laws of planetary motion, publishes *Astronomia Nova*.

Galileo Galilei begins his astronomical observations.

1621

The English mathematician and astronomer Thomas Harriot dies. His only work, *Artis Analyticae Praxis*, is published in 1631.

ca. 1630

The French lawyer and mathematician Pierre de Fermat begins a lifetime of mathematical research. He is the first person to claim to have proved "Fermat's last theorem."

1636

Gérard (or Girard) Desargues, a French mathematician and engineer, publishes *Traité de la section perspective*, which marks the beginning of projective geometry.

1637

René Descartes, a French philosopher and mathematician, publishes *Discours de la méthode*, permanently changing both algebra and geometry.

1638

Galileo Galilei publishes *Dialogues Concerning Two New Sciences* while under arrest.

1640

Blaise Pascal, a French philosopher, scientist, and mathematician, publishes *Essai sur les coniques*, an extension of the work of Desargues.

1642

Blaise Pascal manufactures an early mechanical calculator, the Pascaline.

1648

The Thirty Years' War, a series of conflicts that involves much of Europe, ends.

1649

Oliver Cromwell takes control of the English government after a civil war.

1654

Pierre de Fermat and Blaise Pascal exchange a series of letters about probability, thereby inspiring many mathematicians to study the field.

1655

John Wallis, an English mathematician and clergyman, publishes *Arithmetica Infinitorum*, an important work that presages calculus.

1657

Christian Huygens, a Dutch mathematician, astronomer, and physicist, publishes *De Ratiociniis in Ludo Aleae*, a highly influential text in probability theory.

1662

John Graunt, an English businessman and a pioneer in statistics, publishes his research on the London Bills of Mortality.

1673

Gottfried Leibniz, a German philosopher and mathematician, constructs a mechanical calculator that can perform addition, subtraction, multiplication, division, and extraction of roots.

1683

Seki Kōwa, a Japanese mathematician, discovers the theory of determinants.

1684

Gottfried Leibniz publishes the first paper on calculus, *Nova Methodus pro Maximis et Minimis*.

1687

Isaac Newton, a British mathematician and physicist, publishes *Philosophiae Naturalis Principia Mathematica*, beginning a new era in science.

1693

Edmund Halley, a British mathematician and astronomer, undertakes a statistical study of the mortality rate in Breslau, Germany.

1698

Thomas Savery, an English engineer and inventor, patents the first steam engine.

1705

Jacob Bernoulli, a Swiss mathematician, dies. His major work on probability, *Ars Conjectandi*, is published in 1713.

1712

The first Newcomen steam engine is installed.

1718

Abraham de Moivre, a French mathematician, publishes *The Doctrine of Chances*, the most advanced text of the time on the theory of probability.

1743

The Anglo-Irish Anglican bishop and philosopher George Berkeley publishes *The Analyst*, an attack on the new mathematics pioneered by Isaac Newton and Gottfried Leibniz.

The French mathematician and philosopher Jean Le Rond d'Alembert begins work on the *Encyclopédie*, one of the great works of the Enlightenment.

1748

Leonhard Euler, a Swiss mathematician, publishes his *Introductio*.

1749

The French mathematician and scientist George-Louis Leclerc Buffon publishes the first volume of *Histoire naturelle*.

1750

Gabriel Cramer, a Swiss mathematician, publishes Cramer's rule, a procedure for solving systems of linear equations.

1760

Daniel Bernoulli, a Swiss mathematician and scientist, publishes his probabilistic analysis of the risks and benefits of variolation against smallpox.

Thomas Bayes, an English theologian and mathematician, dies. His "Essay Towards Solving a Problem in the Doctrine of Chances" is published two years later.

1761

The English scientist Joseph Black proposes the idea of latent heat.

1762

Catherine II (Catherine the Great) is proclaimed empress of Russia.

1769

James Watt obtains his first steam engine patent.

1775

American colonists and British troops fight battles at Lexington and Concord, Massachusetts.

1778

Voltaire (François-Marie Arouet), a French writer and philosopher, dies.

1781

William Herschel, a German-born British musician and astronomer, discovers Uranus.

1789

Unrest in France culminates in the French Revolution.

1793

The Reign of Terror, a period of brutal, state-sanctioned repression, begins in France.

1794

The French mathematician Adrien-Marie Legendre (or Le Gendre) publishes his *Éléments de géométrie*, a text that influences mathematics education for decades.

Antoine-Laurent Lavoisier, a French scientist and the discoverer of the law of conservation of matter, is executed by the French government.

1798

Benjamin Thompson (Count Rumford), a British physicist, proposes the equivalence of heat and work.

1799

Napoléon Bonaparte seizes control of the French government.

Caspar Wessel, a Norwegian mathematician and surveyor, publishes the first geometric representation of the complex numbers.

1801

Carl Friedrich Gauss, a German mathematician, publishes *Disquisitiones Arithmeticae*.

1805

Adrien-Marie Le Gendre, a French mathematician, publishes "Nouvelles méthodes pour la détermination des orbites des comètes," which includes the first description of the method of least squares.

1806

Jean-Robert Argand, a French bookkeeper, accountant, and mathematician, develops the Argand diagram to represent complex numbers.

1812

Pierre-Simon Laplace, a French mathematician, publishes *Théorie analytique des probabilite's*, the most influential 19th-century work on the theory of probability.

1815

Napoléon suffers final defeat at the battle of Waterloo.

Jean-Victor Poncelet, a French mathematician and the "father of projective geometry," publishes *Traité des propriétés projectives des figures.*

1824

The French engineer Sadi Carnot publishes *Réflexions,* wherein he describes the Carnot engine.

Niels Henrik Abel, a Norwegian mathematician, publishes his proof of the impossibility of algebraically solving a general fifth-degree equation.

1826

Nikolay Ivanovich Lobachevsky, a Russian mathematician and the "Copernicus of geometry," announces his theory of non-Euclidean geometry.

1828

Robert Brown, a Scottish botanist, publishes the first description of Brownian motion in "A Brief Account of Microscopical Observations."

1830

Charles Babbage, a British mathematician and inventor, begins work on his analytical engine, the first attempt at a modern computer.

1832

János Bolyai, a Hungarian mathematician, publishes *Absolute Science of Space.*

The French mathematician Évariste Galois is killed in a duel.

1843

James Prescott Joule publishes his measurement of the mechanical equivalent of heat.

1846

The planet Neptune is discovered by the French mathematician Urbain-Jean-Joseph Le Verrier from a mathematical analysis of the orbit of Uranus.

1847

Georg Christian von Staudt publishes *Geometrie der Lage*, which shows that projective geometry can be expressed without any concept of length.

1848

Bernhard Bolzano, a Czech mathematician and theologian, dies. His study of infinite sets, *Paradoxien des Unendlichen*, is published in 1851.

1850

Rudolph Clausius, a German mathematician and physicist, publishes his first paper on the theory of heat.

1851

William Thomson (Lord Kelvin), a British scientist, publishes "On the Dynamical Theory of Heat."

1854

George Boole, a British mathematician, publishes *Laws of Thought*. The mathematics contained therein makes possible the later design of computer logic circuits.

The German mathematician Bernhard Riemann gives the historic lecture "On the Hypotheses That Form the Foundations of Geometry." The ideas therein later play an integral part in the theory of relativity.

1855

John Snow, a British physician, publishes "On the Mode of Communication of Cholera," the first successful epidemiological study of a disease.

1859

James Clerk Maxwell, a British physicist, proposes a probabilistic model for the distribution of molecular velocities in a gas.

Charles Darwin, a British biologist, publishes *On the Origin of Species by Means of Natural Selection*.

1861

The American Civil War begins.

1866

The Austrian biologist and monk Gregor Mendel publishes his ideas on the theory of heredity in "Versuche über Pflanzenhybriden."

1867

The Canadian Articles of Confederation unify the British colonies of North America.

1871

Otto von Bismarck is appointed first chancellor of the German Empire.

1872

The German mathematician Felix Klein announces his Erlanger Programme, an attempt to categorize all geometries with the use of group theory.

William Thomson (Lord Kelvin) develops an early analog computer to predict tides.

Richard Dedekind, a German mathematician, rigorously establishes the connection between real numbers and the real number line.

1874

Georg Cantor, a German mathematician, publishes "Über eine Eigenschaft des Inbegriffes aller reelen algebraischen Zahlen," a pioneering paper that shows that not all infinite sets are the same size.

1890

The Hollerith tabulator, an important innovation in calculating machines, is installed at the United States Census for use in the 1890 census.

1899

The German mathematician David Hilbert publishes the definitive axiomatic treatment of Euclidean geometry.

1900

David Hilbert announces his list of mathematics problems for the 20th century.

The Russian mathematician Andrey Andreyevich Markov begins his research into the theory of probability.

1901

Henri-Léon Lebesgue, a French mathematician, develops his theory of integration.

1905

Ernst Zermelo, a German mathematician, undertakes the task of axiomatizing set theory.

Albert Einstein, a German-born American physicist, begins to publish his discoveries in physics.

1906

Marian Smoluchowski, a Polish scientist, publishes his insights into Brownian motion.

1908

The Hardy-Weinberg law, containing ideas fundamental to population genetics, is published.

1910

Bertrand Russell, a British logician and philosopher, and Alfred North Whitehead, a British mathematician and philosopher, publish *Principia Mathematica*, an important work on the foundations of mathematics.

1914

World War I begins.

1917

Vladimir Ilyich Lenin leads a revolution that results in the founding of the Union of Soviet Socialist Republics.

1918

World War I ends.

The German mathematician Emmy Noether presents her ideas on the roles of symmetries in physics.

1929

Andrey Nikolayevich Kolmogorov, a Russian mathematician, publishes *General Theory of Measure and Probability Theory*, establishing the theory of probability on a firm axiomatic basis for the first time.

1930

Ronald Aylmer Fisher, a British geneticist and statistician, publishes *Genetical Theory of Natural Selection*, an important early attempt to express the theory of natural selection in mathematics.

1931

Kurt Gödel, an Austrian-born American mathematician, publishes his incompleteness proof.

The Differential Analyzer, an important development in analog computers, is developed at Massachusetts Institute of Technology.

1933

Karl Pearson, a British innovator in statistics, retires from University College, London.

1935

George Horace Gallup, a U.S. statistician, founds the American Institute of Public Opinion.

1937

The British mathematician Alan Turing publishes his insights on the limits of computability.

1939

World War II begins.

William Edwards Deming joins the United States Census Bureau.

1945

World War II ends.

1946

The Electronic Numerical Integrator and Calculator (ENIAC) computer begins operation at the University of Pennsylvania.

1948

While working at Bell Telephone Labs in the United States, Claude Shannon publishes "A Mathematical Theory of Communication," marking the beginning of the Information Age.

1951

The Universal Automatic Computer (UNIVAC I) is installed at U.S. Bureau of the Census.

1954

FORmula TRANslator (Fortran), one of the first high-level computer languages, is introduced.

1956

The American Walter Shewhart, an innovator in the field of quality control, retires from Bell Telephone Laboratories.

1957

Olga Oleinik publishes "Discontinuous Solutions to Nonlinear Differential Equations," a milestone in mathematical physics.

1964

IBM Corporation introduces the IBM System/360 computer for government agencies and large businesses.

1965

Andrey Nikolayevich Kolmogorov establishes the branch of mathematics now known as Kolmogorov complexity.

1966

A Programming Language (APL) computer language is implemented on the IBM System/360 computer.

1972

Amid much fanfare the French mathematician and philosopher René Thom establishes a new field of mathematics called catastrophe theory.

1973

The C computer language, developed at Bell Laboratories, is essentially completed.

1975

The French geophysicist Jean Morlet helps develop a new kind of analysis based on what he calls wavelets.

1977

Digital Equipment Corporation introduces the VAX computer.

1981

IBM Corporation introduces the IBM personal computer (PC).

1989

The Belgian mathematician Ingrid Daubechies develops what has become the mathematical foundation for today's wavelet research.

1991

The Union of Soviet Socialist Republics dissolves into 15 separate nations.

1995

The British mathematician Andrew Wiles publishes the first proof of Fermat's last theorem.

Cray Research introduces the CRAY E-1200, a machine that sustains a rate of one terraflop (1 trillion calculations per second) on real-world applications.

JAVA computer language is introduced commercially by Sun Microsystems.

1997

René Thom declares the mathematical field of catastrophe theory "dead."

2002

Experimental Mathematics celebrates its 10th anniversary. It is a refereed journal dedicated to the experimental aspects of mathematical research.

Manindra Agrawal, Neeraj Kayal, and Nitin Saxena create a brief, elegant algorithm to test whether a number is prime, thereby solving an important centuries-old problem.

2003

Grigory Perelman produces what may be the first complete proof of the Poincaré conjecture, a statement on the most fundamental properties of three-dimensional shapes.

GLOSSARY

axiom a statement accepted as true that serves as a basis for deductive reasoning

calculus the branch of mathematics that is based on the ideas and techniques of differentiation and integration. The techniques of calculus have enabled researchers to solve many new problems in mathematics and physics

caloric a hypothetical form of matter (now known not to exist) that was thought to be responsible for heat

Carnot engine a theoretical heat engine that establishes a bound on the efficiency of all heat engines operating between any two thermal reservoirs at given temperatures

celestial sphere an imaginary sphere—with Earth at or near its center—against which the stars seem to be projected

classical physics the branch of physics composed of logical consequences of the laws of conservation of momentum, mass, and energy as they were first proposed in the 17th, 18th, and 19th centuries

conservation of energy the physical principle that the total energy of any isolated system remains constant

conservation law the statement that a physical property, such as energy, is preserved over the course of a transformation or process provided that the system in which the transformation occurs is isolated from its surroundings

conservation of mass the physical principle that in an isolated system (in the absence of nuclear reactions) the mass of the system remains constant

conservation of momentum   the physical principle that the total momentum of an isolated system remains constant

convergent series   an infinite series of numbers with the property that the sum of the first n terms of the series approaches a unique number as the value of n tends toward infinity

continuity equation   the mathematical statement that in an isolated system a fluid's mass is a conserved property

derivative   the limit of a ratio formed by the difference in the dependent variable to the difference in the independent variable as the difference in the independent variable tends toward 0

differential equation   an equation containing the derivatives of an unknown function. The solution of a differential equation is the function or functions whose derivatives satisfy the equation and any subsidiary conditions

differentiation   the act of computing a derivative

DNA (deoxyribonucleic acid)   the molecule of heredity; the mechanism that encodes all of the information required to enable a cell to develop into an individual organism

ecliptic   the circle formed by the intersection of the celestial sphere and the plane containing the Earth's orbital path

efficiency   in thermodynamics the work performed by a cyclic heat engine per cycle divided by the amount of heat absorbed per cycle expressed as a percentage; the closer this quotient is to 100 percent, the more efficient the engine

ellipse   a closed curve obtained by the intersection of a right circular cone and a plane

entropy   a measure of the amount of energy in a physical system that is unavailable to do work

first law of thermodynamics   the assertion that energy is a conserved property

fluid dynamics   the branch of physics that deals with the properties of liquids and gases in motion

gene   the basic unit of biological inheritance. A single gene controls the production or expression of a single protein

Hardy-Weinberg law   a fundamental principle of population genetics that states sufficient conditions for the stability of gene frequencies from one generation to the next. There are six conditions: (1) The population must be very large; (2) reproduction occurs randomly; (3) there is no migration into or out of the population; (4) there are no differential survival rates; (5) the number of offspring produced does not vary between individuals or between reproducing pairs of individuals; (6) the genes do not mutate

heat   energy that is transferred from one body to another as a result of a temperature difference between the two bodies

heliostatic model   the model of the solar system that states that the Sun is motionless and that the planets orbit a point that is not necessarily the center of the Sun

infinitesimal analysis   the branch of mathematics from which calculus developed. It involves the manipulation of quantities that are "infinitesimal," or incalculably small

integration   the ideas and techniques belonging to calculus that are used in computing the lengths of curves, the size of areas, and the volumes of solids

invariant   unchanged by a particular set of mathematical or physical transformations

Kepler's laws of planetary motion   three statements formulated by Johannes Kepler that describe the motion of planets about the Sun

latent heat   heat that, when transferred from one body to another, results in a change of phase rather than a change of temperature

law of gravity   the description of how the gravitational force exerted between two bodies depends upon the distance between them and their masses. The law of gravity states that the strength of the gravitational force exerted between two bodies is proportional to the product of the masses of the bodies and inversely proportional to the square of the distance between them

laws of heredity   the basic principles that describe how traits are passed from one generation to the next as well as how those traits are expressed. These laws were first formulated by Gregor Mendel. In modern terminology Mendel asserted that (1) heredity is particulate, that is, there exists a basic unit of inheritance—now called a gene; (2) each organism inherits one copy of each gene from each parent; and (3) genes on different chromosomes are inherited independently of one another. Mendel went on to describe the ways different forms of the same gene were expressed in an individual

laws of motion   three statements, first formulated in their entirety by Isaac Newton, that describe the ways forces affect motions: (1) A body maintains its state of rest or of uniform motion unless acted upon by an external force; (2) the change in momentum of a body is proportional to the strength of the force acting on it and is made in the direction in which the force is impressed; (3) forces occur in pairs; when body A exerts a force on body B, body B exerts a force that is equal in magnitude and opposite in direction on body A

mechanical equivalent of heat   the statement that a given amount of work is always equivalent to a particular amount of heat energy, specifically: 4.18 Joules of mechanical energy equals 1 calorie of heat energy

momentum   the physical property of a body that equals the mass of the body times its velocity

mutation   random change in the genetic makeup of an organism

parabola   the curve formed by the intersection of a right circular cone and a plane when the plane is parallel to a line that generates the cone

phase   the physical state of matter. Matter generally occurs in one of three phases: liquid, solid, or gas

Platonic solids   the set of five regular solids consisting of the tetrahedron, the octahedron, the cube, the dodecahedron, and the icosahedron

population genetics   the branch of genetics that seeks to quantify the amount of genetic variability present in a population of organisms as well as the causes of that variability and its rate of change in response to environmental factors

postulate   see AXIOM

protein   a complex chain of amino acids joined together

reservoir, thermal   a source of heat with the following two properties: (1) It is at the same temperature throughout; (2) the heat source holds so much heat that its temperature remains very nearly constant when it is used in the operation of a heat engine

retrograde motion   the apparent west-to-east motion of the planets as viewed from Earth

second law of thermodynamics   the assertion, fundamental to science, that a process whose only end result is to transfer heat from a body at lower temperature to one at a higher temperature is impossible

sensible heat   heat that results in a change in temperature rather than a change in phase

statics   the branch of physics that deals with bodies under the action of forces that are in equilibrium

station   in astronomy a location in the sky where the apparent motion of a planet across the background stars seems to cease

symmetry   a particular type of invariance expressed in physical and geometrical phenomena. Objects and phenomena exhibit symmetry with respect to a transformation, such as reflection about a line or plane, when that transformation leaves the spatial configuration of the object or phenomenon unchanged. Symmetry can also be defined for the equations that describe objects or phenomena

tangent   the best straight-line approximation to a smoothly varying curve at a given point

thermodynamics   the branch of physics that deals with the convertability of heat into work and vice versa

zodiac   a band of sky centered on the ecliptic that contains the apparent path of every planet except Pluto when viewed from Earth

FURTHER READING

MODERN WORKS

Boyer, Carl B., and Uta C. Merzbach. *A History of Mathematics.* New York: John Wiley & Sons, 1991. Boyer was one of the preeminent mathematics historians of the 20th century. This work contains much interesting biographical information. The mathematical information assumes a fairly strong background of the reader.

Bruno, Leonard C. *Math and Mathematicians: The History of Mathematics Discoveries around the World,* 2 vols. Detroit, Mich.: U·X·L, 1999. Despite its name there is little mathematics in this two-volume set. What you will find is a very large number of brief biographies of many individuals who were important in the history of mathematics.

Courant, Richard, and Herbert Robbins. *What Is Mathematics? An Elementary Approach to Ideas and Mathematics.* New York: Oxford University Press, 1941. A classic and exhaustive answer to the question posed in the title. Courant was an important and influential 20th-century mathematician.

Davis, Phillip J. *The Lore of Large Numbers.* New York: Random House, 1961. An excellent overview of numbers, how they are written, and how they are used in science.

Dewdney, Alexander K. *200% of Nothing: An Eye-Opening Tour through the Twists and Turns of Math Abuse and Innumeracy.* New York: John Wiley & Sons, 1993. A critical look at how mathematical reasoning has been abused to distort truth.

Eastaway, Robert, and Jeremy Wyndham. *Why Do Buses Come in Threes? The Hidden Mathematics of Everyday Life.* New York: John Wiley & Sons, 1998. Nineteen lighthearted essays on the mathematics underlying everything from luck to scheduling problems.

Eves, Howard. *An Introduction to the History of Mathematics.* New York: Holt, Rinehart & Winston, 1953. This well-written history of mathematics places special emphasis on early mathematics. It is unusual because the history is accompanied by numerous mathematical problems. (The solutions are in the back of the book.)

Freudenthal, Hans. *Mathematics Observed.* New York: McGraw-Hill, 1967. A collection of seven survey articles about math topics from computability to geometry to physics (some more technical than others).

Gardner, M. *The Ambidextrous Universe: Mirror Asymmetry and Time-Reversed Worlds.* New York: Scribner's, 1979. A readable look at geometric transformations and their physical meaning.

———. *The Colossal Book of Mathematics.* New York: Norton, 2001. Martin Gardner had a gift for seeing things mathematically. This "colossal" book contains sections on geometry, algebra, probability, logic, and more.

Guillen, Michael. *Bridges to Infinity: The Human Side of Mathematics.* Los Angeles: Jeremy P. Tarcher, 1983. This book consists of an engaging nontechnical set of essays on mathematical topics, including non-Euclidean geometry, transfinite numbers, and catastrophe theory.

Heath, Thomas L. *A History of Greek Mathematics.* New York: Dover Publications, 1981. First published early in the 20th century and reprinted numerous times, this book is still one of the main references on the subject.

Kline, Morris. *Mathematics and the Physical World.* New York: Thomas Y. Crowell, 1959. The history of mathematics as it relates to the history of science and vice versa.

———. *Mathematics for the Nonmathematician.* New York: Dover Publications, 1985. An articulate, not very technical overview of many important mathematical ideas.

———. *Mathematics in Western Culture.* New York: Oxford University Press, 1953. An excellent overview of the development of Western mathematics in its cultural context, this book is aimed at an audience with a firm grasp of high school–level mathematics.

Mlodinow, Leonard. *Euclid's Window: The Story of Geometry from Parallel Lines to Hyperspace*. New York: The Free Press, 2001. An interesting narrative about the interplay between geometry and our views of the universe from Thales to the present.

North, John. *The Norton History of Astronomy and Cosmology*. New York: Norton, 1995. The early sections of this book contain an overview of the geometrical astronomy of the Mesopotamians and Greeks.

Packel, Edward W. *The Mathematics of Games and Gambling*. Washington, D.C.: Mathematical Association of America, 1981. A well-written introduction to probability theory and random phenomena expressed in the language of games.

Pappas, Theoni. *The Joy of Mathematics*. San Carlos, Calif.: World Wide/Tetra, 1986. Aimed at a younger audience, this work searches for interesting applications of mathematics in the world around us.

Pierce, John R. *An Introduction to Information Theory: Symbols, Signals and Noise*. New York: Dover Publications, 1961. Despite the sound of the title, this is not a textbook. Pierce, formerly of Bell Laboratories, describes (among other topics) how entropy in physics is related to the concept of uncertainty in information theory.

Rucker, Rudy V. B. *The Fourth Dimension: Toward a Geometry of Higher Reality*. Boston: Houghton Mifflin, 1984. A clever examination of ideas associated with geometry and perception.

Sawyer, Walter W. *What Is Calculus About?* New York: Random House, 1961. A highly readable description of a sometimes intimidating, historically important subject. Absolutely no calculus background required.

Schiffer, M., and Leon Bowden. *The Role of Mathematics in Science*. Washington, D.C.: Mathematical Association of America, 1984. The first few chapters of this book, ostensibly written for high school students, will be accessible to many students; the last few chapters will find a much narrower audience.

Spangenburg, Ray, and Diane K. Moser. *Modern Science: 1896–1945*. New York: Facts On File, 2004. Background on scientific ideas that motivated much of the mathematics of the 20th century.

Spangenburg, Ray, and Diane K. Moser. *The Age of Synthesis: 1800–1895*. New York: Facts On File, 2004. Background on scientific ideas that motivated much of the mathematics of the 19th century.

Stewart, Ian. *From Here to Infinity*. New York: Oxford University Press, 1996. A well-written, very readable overview of several important contemporary ideas in geometry, algebra, computability, chaos, and mathematics in nature.

———. *Life's Other Secret: The New Mathematics of the Living World*. New York: John Wiley, 1998. As mathematics broadens its scope from the physical sciences to the biological sciences, new mathematical ideas will be developed. This book describes some of those ideas.

Swetz, Frank J., editor. *From Five Fingers to Infinity: A Journey through the History of Mathematics*. Chicago: Open Court, 1994. This is a fascinating, though not especially focused look at the history of mathematics. Highly recommended.

Tabak, John. *The History of Mathematics: Geometry*. New York: Facts On File, 2004. More information about the relationships that exist between geometry and our perception of the world around us.

———. *A Look at Neptune*. New York: Franklin Watts, 2003. Primarily for younger readers, this book also contains a demonstration of the way the mass of Neptune can be calculated from observations of the motion of its moon, Triton.

———. *History of Mathematics. Probability and Statistics*. New York: Facts On File, 2004. More information about the relationships that exist between the idea of randomness and the natural world.

Yaglom, Isaac M. *Geometric Transformations*, translated by Allen Shields. New York: Random House, 1962. Aimed at high school students, this is a very sophisticated treatment of "simple" geometry and an excellent introduction to higher mathematics. It is also an excellent introduction to the concept of invariance.

Yoler, Yusuf A. *Perception of Natural Events by Human Observers*. Bellevue, Wash.: Unipress, 1993. Sections one and three of this book give a nice overview of the geometry that is a consequence of the theory of relativity.

ORIGINAL SOURCES

Reading the discoverer's own description can sometimes deepen our appreciation of an important mathematical discovery. Often this is not possible, because the description is too technical. Fortunately there are exceptions. Sometimes the discovery is accessible because the idea does not require a lot of technical background to appreciate it; sometimes the discoverer writes a nontechnical account of the technical idea that she or he has discovered. Here are some classic papers:

Archimedes. *The Method Treating of Mechanical Problems.* Translated by Sir Thomas Heath. *Great Books of the Western World.* Vol. 11. Chicago: Encyclopaedia Britannica, 1952. Archimedes' own account of his method for discovering mathematical truth.

Archimedes. *On the Equilibrium of Planes, or The Centres of Gravity of Planes I and II.* Translated by Sir Thomas L. Heath. *Great Books of the Western World.* Vol. 11. Chicago: Encyclopaedia Britannica, 1952. This is a beautiful example of applying mathematical methods to the study of physics by one of the great mathematicians in history.

Copernicus, Nicolaus. *On the Revolutions of the Heavenly Spheres.* Translated by Charles Glenn Wallis. *Great Books of the Western World.* Vol. 16. Chicago: Encyclopaedia Britannica, 1952. This book changed the world. It is filled with tables, diagrams, explanations, and a surprising amount of mysticism.

Galilei, Galileo. *Dialogues Concerning Two New Sciences.* Translated by Henry Crew and Alfonso de Salvio. New York: Dover Publications, 1954. An interesting literary work as well as a pioneering physics text. Many regard the publication of this text as the beginning of the modern scientific tradition.

———. *Discoveries and Opinions of Galileo.* Translated by Stillman Drake. New York: Doubleday Anchor Books, 1957. A collection of short and influential works by Galileo. In the article "The Assayer" you can read Galileo's arguments for the adoption of the scientific method and against reliance on ancient authorities. His ideas have since become an integral part of our culture.

Hardy, Godfrey H. *A Mathematician's Apology.* Cambridge, England: Cambridge University Press, 1940. Hardy was an excellent mathematician and a good writer. In this oft-quoted and very brief book Hardy seeks to explain and sometimes justify his life as a mathematician.

Kepler, Johannes. *Epitome of Copernican Astronomy IV and V.* Translated by Charles Glenn Wallis. *Great Books of the Western World.* Vol. 16. Chicago: Encyclopaedia Britannica, 1952. Written in the form of a long series of questions and answers, Kepler's *Epitome* helped create a new era in astronomy.

———. *The Harmonies of the World V.* Translated by Charles Glenn Wallis. *Great Books of the Western World.* Vol. 16. Chicago: Encyclopaedia Britannica, 1952. Platonic solids, music, and mysticism are all employed in the study of astronomy. This early work by Kepler straddles the boundary between the old and new ways of thinking about science.

Mendel, Gregor. "Mathematics of Heredity." In *The World of Mathematics.* Vol. 2, edited by James R. Newman. New York: Dover Publications, 1956. Here, in Mendel's own words, is a description of how he discovered the laws of heredity. This account is a remarkable example of imagination and scientific determination.

Newton, Isaac. *Mathematical Principles of Natural Philosophy.* Translated by Andrew Motte, revised by Florian Cajori. *Great Books of the Western World.* Vol. 34. Chicago: Encyclopaedia Britannica, 1952. Some of this book is written for experts, but some is quite accessible. See especially the section "Axioms or Laws of Motion" for a classic example of how to apply mathematical methods to the study of physical science.

Ptolemy. *The Almagest.* Translated by R. Catesby Taliaferro. *Great Books of the Western World.* Vol. 16. Chicago: Encyclopaedia Britannica, 1952. Filled with diagrams, tables, and explanations, this is one of the most important astronomical texts in history and an important example of ancient science.

Stevin, Simon. *Principal Works.* Edited by Ernes Crane et al.; translated by C. Dikshoorn. 5 vols. Amsterdam: C. V. Swets and Zeitlinger,

1955–66. Every history of mathematics devotes space to Simon Stevin, but unlike those of Galileo and Kepler, Stevin's writings are difficult to find. This very readable translation is available in some larger libraries.

Weyl, Hermann. "Symmetry." In *The World of Mathematics*. Vol. 1, edited by James R. Newman. New York: Dover Publications, 1956. An extended meditation on a geometric idea that has become a central organizing principle in contemporary physics by a pioneer in the subject.

INTERNET RESOURCES

Athena Earth and Space Science for K–12. Available on-line. URL: http://inspire.ospi.wednet.edu:8001/. Updated May 13, 1999. Funded by NASA's Public Use of Remote Sensing Data, this site contains many interesting applications of mathematics to the study of natural phenomena.

Beretta, Marco, Andrea Scotti, Daniele Nuzzo, Pietro Corsi, Raphaël Bange. The Project, Panopticon Lavoisier. Available on-line. URL: http://moro.imss.fi.it/lavoisier/entrance/projbox.html. Downloaded June 3, 2003. A beautifully crafted website devoted entirely to Lavoisier and his accomplishments.

The Eisenhower National Clearinghouse for Mathematics and Science Education. Available on-line. URL: http://www.enc.org/. Downloaded June 2, 2003. As its name implies, this site is a clearinghouse for a comprehensive set of links to interesting sites in math and science.

Electronic Bookshelf. Available on-line. URL: http://hilbert.dartmouth.edu/~matc/eBookshelf/art/index.html. Updated May 21, 2002. This site is maintained by Dartmouth College. It is both visually beautiful and informative, and it has links to many creative presentations on computer science, the history of mathematics, and mathematics. It also treats a number of other topics from a mathematical perspective.

Eric Weisstein's World of Mathematics. Available on-line. URL: http://mathworld.wolfram.com/. Updated April 10, 2002. This site has brief overviews of a great many topics in mathematics. The level of presentation varies substantially from topic to topic.

Faber, Vance, Bonnie Yantis, Mike Hawrylycz, Nancy Casey, Mike Fellows, Mike Barnett, Gretchen Wissner. This is MEGA Mathematics! Available on-line. URL: http://www.c3.lanl.gov/mega-math. Downloaded June 2, 2003. Maintained by the Los Alamos National Laboratories, one of the premier scientific establishments in the world, this site has a number of unusual offerings. It is well worth a visit.

Fife, Earl, and Larry Husch. Math Archives. "History of Mathematics." Available on-line. URL: http://archives.math.utk.edu/topics/history.html. Updated January 2002. Information on mathematics, mathematicians, and mathematical organizations.

Gangolli, Ramesh. *Asian Contributions to Mathematics.* Available on-line. URL: http://www.pps.k12.or.us/depts-c/mc-me/be-as-ma.pdf. Downloaded June 2, 2003. As its name implies, this well-written on-line book focuses on the history of mathematics in Asia and its influence on the world history of mathematics. It also includes information on the work of Asian Americans, a welcome contribution to the field.

The Math Forum @ Drexel. The Math Forum Student Center. Available on-line. URL: http://mathforum.org/students/. Updated June 2, 2003. Probably the best website for information about the mathematics that students encounter in their school-related studies. You will find interesting and challenging problems and solutions for students in grades K–12 as well as a fair amount of college-level information.

Melville, Duncan J. Mesopotamian Mathematics. Available on-line. URL: http://it.stlawu.edu/ca.dmelvill/mesomath/. Updated March 17, 2003. This creative site is devoted to many aspects of Mesopotamian mathematics. It also has a link to a "cuneiform calculator," which can be fun to use.

O'Connor, John L., and Edmund F. Robertson. The MacTutor History of Mathematics Archive. Available on-line. URL: http://www–gap.dcs.st-and.ac.uk/~history/index.html. Updated May 2003. This is a valuable resource for anyone interested in

learning more about the history of mathematics. It contains an extraordinary collection of biographies of mathematicians in different cultures and times. In addition it provides information about the historical development of certain key mathematical ideas.

PERIODICALS, THROUGH THE MAIL AND ON-LINE

+Plus

URL: http://pass.maths.org.uk
A site with numerous interesting articles about all aspects of high school math. They send an email every few weeks to their subscribers to keep them informed about new articles at the site.

Function

Business Manager
Department of Mathematics and Statistics
Monash University
Victoria 3800
Australia
function@maths.monash.edu.au
Published five times per year, this refereed journal is aimed at older high school students.

The Math Goodies Newsletter

http://www.mathgoodies.com/newsletter/
A popular, free e-newsletter that is sent out twice per month.

Parabola: A Mathematics Magazine for Secondary Students

Australian Mathematics Trust
University of Canberra
ACT 2601
Australia

Published twice a year by the Australian Mathematics Trust in association with the University of New South Wales, *Parabola* is a source of short high-quality articles on many aspects of mathematics. Some back issues are also available free on-line. See URL: http://www.maths.unsw.edu.au/Parabola/index.html.

Pi in the Sky

http://www.pims.math.ca/pi/
Part of the Pacific Institute for the Mathematical Sciences, this high school mathematics magazine is available over the Internet.

Scientific American

415 Madison Avenue
New York, NY 10017
A serious and widely read monthly magazine, *Scientific American* regularly carries high-quality articles on mathematics and mathematically intensive branches of science. This is the one "popular" source of high-quality mathematical information that you will find at a newsstand.

INDEX

Italic page numbers indicate illustrations.